FREUD AND
THE DILEMMAS OF PSYCHOLOGY

FREUD AND THE DILEMMAS OF PSYCHOLOGY

by

MARIE JAHODA

BASIC BOOKS Inc.

PUBLISHERS, NEW YORK

Library of Congress Catalog Card Number: 76–46853

ISBN: 0–465–02561–7

Printed in Great Britain

Contents

Acknowledgements

I HAVE tried to acknowledge my intellectual debts to the psychological and psychoanalytic literature—I hope without cryptomnesia—in the notes to the text; there are too many to enumerate them here. In addition, several persons were kind enough to read an earlier version of this book and I have profited as much from their criticisms as from their encouragement. I wish to record my special thanks to Austen Albu who by virtue of a privileged position did not mince his words; to Gustav Kuerti who though somewhat less privileged was equally frank; to Neil Warren who over a distance of several thousand miles continued a long-standing dialogue and drew my attention to contributions which I might otherwise have overlooked; to two former students, Howard Rush and John Moulton; to John Bailyn for his help in constructing the index; and to Veronica Craig-Mair who added pertinent comment to her secretarial skills.

I am grateful to Sigmund Freud Copyrights Ltd, The Hogarth Press Ltd, and The Institute of Psycho-Analysis for permission to quote from *The Standard Edition of the Complete Psychological Works of Sigmund Freud*, revised and edited by James Strachey.

M.J.

INTRODUCTION

An Unfinished Debate

THREE-QUARTERS of a century after the publication of *The Interpretation of Dreams* Freud's place in man's intellectual enterprises is still unsettled. That he has a place is beyond controversy. The question is: where? A seemingly unending flood of publications provides contradictory answers: a scientist or a charlatan; the founder of a new psychology or a poet; a philosopher or a philosopher manqué; a positivist or a metaphysician; a biological or a social determinist; a moralist or a libertarian; an original thinker or a clever propagandist of other people's ideas; an organiser of a movement or a lonely pioneer; a curse or a blessing for science and morality.

There is surely an intriguing intellectual puzzle here: what keeps the controversy over Freud alive and so heated? Why cannot scholars, who to their own satisfaction 'proved' decades ago that 'what was new in Freud was not true, and what was true was not new', let go of the attack?

Controversy about ideas is, of course, commonplace. But there is a special slant to the controversy over Freud. In the case of Darwin or Marx it was the Darwinists and the Marxists who led the fight for the new ideas; in the case of Freud the psychoanalysts are on the defensive, most of them restricting themselves to their professional practice and emerging from their sect-like existence only occasionally to answer some new accusation. If it depended on them, Freud's name would no longer be a battlecry in contemporary intellectual issues, such as the critical stage in which psychology finds itself today, or the women's liberation movement; but it still is and the debate continues.

Of course, this is not to imply that psychoanalysts are epigones only. Since Freud's death, and even before, they have produced a truly phenomenal volume of literature, clarifying and developing Freud's work, both clinically and theoretically. The *Index of Psychoanalytic Writings*,[1] listing every psychoanalytic book, article or monograph in twenty-one languages, has now passed the 100,000 mark. While it would be wrong to pretend that I know more than a small fraction of these works, what I do know suggests two points: first, psychoanalysts write largely for other psychoanalysts; and second, however innovating or critical their ideas, virtually all of them take Freud as their starting point. This latter feature extends also to those schools of psychotherapy, neo-Freudians and others, which have deliberately and sometimes vituperatively broken away from Freud. This book too will concentrate on Freud's own work, for in agreement with his followers and his critics I regard his contribution as the centre of the unfinished debate about the intellectual status of psychoanalysis. However promising or outrageous the work of some contemporary psychoanalysts may be, none of them has had a comparable impact, none has created a comparable controversy.

This book is written under no illusion of ending this controversy. On the contrary, from the perspective of a psychologist, aware of the fact that the attack against Freud is fiercest among psychologists, it should be kept alive.

When I first became a student of psychology at the University of Vienna in the late 1920's, my teacher, Karl Bühler, published a book entitled *Die Krise der Psychologie*. His work remained strangely unappreciated when the Anglo-Saxon world became the centre of psychological thought. The crisis lingered on, partially disguised by successive fashions in psychological thought and some remarkable achievements. Now it is out in the open again. Over half a century my conviction has deepened that the very existence of Freud's thought is a thorn in the flesh of academic psychology that should not be prematurely removed. The study of Freud cannot yet be left to the historians of ideas. It still has a function to fill for the development of psychology.

This is why this book is written for psychologists, in the hope that an exposition and appraisal of Freud's work may make a contribution to the clarification of the issues with which psychology is struggling.

There are, of course, already a large number of such efforts in existence, some of them excellent even though partisan, some of them excellent even though without a point of view, and others of doubtful quality. Although I have learned a great deal from them they do not suit my particular bias: the presentation of Freud's thought in awareness both of his critics and of the problems of psychology as a science. In any case, the existence of such works has not yet produced a consistent view of Freud among psychologists. Quite recently on the same day I came across papers by two psychologists, one referring to him as a biological determinist, the other as an environmentalist.

One explanation for the confusion about 'what Freud really said' is that he contradicts himself. The reader of the psychological literature should not be misled into thinking that Freud had a consistent position. The absence of contradictions would be truly astounding, given the sheer volume of his work. The now completed *Standard Edition** of Freud's collected psychological works has 24 volumes, but excludes not only his early physiological and neurological papers, but also his voluminous correspondence which was to a large extent concerned with the intellectual problems of psychoanalysis. It would be unreasonable to expect every psychologist actively involved in the study of his subject to burrow his way through this mountain of material.

Given the amount and complexity of Freud's thought, its exposition is inevitably always incomplete, selective and immensely difficult. Freud himself bears testimony to this. On various occasions he tried to present psychoanalysis systematically, most notably perhaps in the *Introductory* and *New Introductory Lectures on Psychoanalysis*. None of these efforts was

*All references to Freud's work are to this *Standard Edition of the Complete Psychological Works of Sigmund Freud*, translated and published under the editorship of James Strachey, in collaboration with Anna Freud and with the assistance of Alix Strachey, Alan Tyson and Angela Richards (London, The Hogarth Press).

satisfactory. He must have thought so himself, otherwise he would not have tried again and again to the very end of his life when there remained incomplete, and published posthumously, the *Outline of Psychoanalysis*. Important though these works are, they contain neither all the assumptions and changes in his thought, nor the contradictions, inconsistencies and lacunae in the detailed body of his work. It is true, Philip Rieff[2] called Freud 'the least confused of modern minds because he has no message; he accepts contradictions'. While one can agree with this statement it adds to the difficulty of exposition.

Another reason for the difficulty of the task stems, perhaps paradoxically, from the fact that some acquaintance with his thought is enormously widespread. This vulgarised version of psychoanalysis, which twenty years ago Trilling called 'the slang of our culture',[3] has become so deeply engrained in the hearsay knowledge of Freudian thought, even among some psychologists, that it requires a particular effort to redress the balance in these all too well prepared minds. Freud himself was keenly aware of the dangers inherent in popular success. In a preface to a book by de Saussure, he thanked him explicitly for his correction of the widespread view that according to psychoanalysis all dreams have a sexual meaning, and that sex is the only motive power in man. Neither statement was, of course, ever made by Freud.

All these are weighty reasons against trying, once again, to confront psychologists with Freud's thought. Obviously the effort seems worthwhile to me. I can only hope that it will seem so to the reader as well.

CHAPTER 1

The Scope of the Controversy

THERE is virtually no aspect of Freud's work that has escaped becoming the subject of controversy; even some biographical details provided by him or his contemporaries are now open to doubt. To describe and discuss them exhaustively would fill a volume in itself; a few selected examples, however, can at least indicate the range of these controversies.

Since Ernest Jones's monumental biography[1] Freud scholarship has taken a dramatic upswing; documents are sifted and sorted, and contradictory assertions abound. Jones tells us that Freud was born in 1856, as the first son of Jacob Freud's second marriage. There is no controversy about the date, but was it Jacob's second marriage? No, says Ellenberger, in his magnificent and scholarly work, it was the third.[2] The question is: does it matter? Scholarship applied to the lives of great men can easily veer from the sublime to the ridiculous. There is a (perhaps apocryphal) anecdote about an early edition of Goethe's autobiography. Goethe wrote: 'Of all the women I loved, I loved Lili most', with a footnote by the editor: 'Hier irrt Goethe' (here Goethe is wrong). But in Freud's case the situation is different for he has, as it were, given us permission to consider his personal experiences as data. *The Interpretation of Dreams*[3] contains an account of his self-analysis, and in many other writings he has used his own personal experience ruthlessly and revealingly to demonstrate the workings of the mind, much in contrast to some other psychologists whose work explains everybody but themselves.

The controversy over biographical details matters, some maintain, because they are relevant to the question of whether Freud's work was based on adequate reality testing or on the distortions of a neurotic mind. The family drama in early childhood is, after all, central to Freud's thought. His first conception of its nature emerged from his self-analysis. Freud's parental family had a peculiar composition, even on the assumption that his mother was Jacob's second wife. How much more so if there was a family secret apparently never mentioned publicly but, as is the wont of all family secrets, colouring the atmosphere, emerging in vague allusions and feeding the fantasy life of the young. The facts of this matter can probably be established beyond doubt; its possible impact on Freud must forever remain a matter of speculation.

In his autobiographical sketch,[4] in *The Interpretation* and in his correspondence, Freud mentions three related experiences which had profound effects on him: anti-Semitism, his frustration over the delay in his academic promotion, and his loneliness and exposure to hostility in the first decade of his psychoanalytical discoveries. All three have become subject to controversy.

Freud reports that when he was a young schoolboy his father once told him how he had been humiliated by a Gentile in the street who threw his cap in the mud and forced him off the pavement. Much like the young generation of Israeli Jews during the Eichman trial who were shocked to learn of their parents' submission to humiliation even before torture, the young Freud was shocked by what he regarded as his father's cowardice in the incident. For generations it has been the fate of Jews to live with the knowledge of humiliation in the previous generation, to regard it as past history, and to have to live through it once again. In Freud's case the full terror came later when he had to leave Vienna in 1938. Four of his sisters who could not flee with him perished in concentration camps. But throughout the period of his active working life in Vienna he was aware of anti-Semitism and attributed to it some of the resistance to his work and the delay in his promotion to a professorship. Ellenberger[2] regards Freud's statements in this respect as exaggerations, typical of the hypersensitivity of many Jews; he regards the period of about 1880–1910 as one in which 'anti-Semitism was practically non-existent in Vienna' (p. 424); and 'Freud had in common with some Austrian Jews his extreme sensitivity to any (true or supposed) form of anti-Semitism' (p. 427). He concludes that the major reason for the delay in Freud's nomination was the bureaucratic *vis inertiae* (p. 454).

Other scholars provided the documentation for this controversy. The Gicklhorns[5] wrote a book on Freud's academic career in the light of documents which supports Ellenberger, while K. R. Eissler[6] answered it by producing two documents they had overlooked which support Freud's interpretation.

Now there can be no conceivable doubt that Austrian society contained the canker of anti-Semitism throughout Freud's lifetime, long before it produced the catastrophe of the twentieth century. In 1895 Dr. Karl Lueger became mayor of Vienna, whose anti-Semitism is as well attested as its modification by his famous statement 'Wer ein Jud ist, bestimm ich' (I decide who is a Jew). But his political friends were beyond such modifications. In 1900 a member of the Austrian parliament published a pamphlet[7] which was an effort in futurology and described the history of Vienna viewed from the year 1920. It contains the following statement:

> 'In Vienna we once hanged 300 Jews and 20 Aryans in one day. In the Polish and Ruthenian states we had to hang thousands before the villains realized we were serious.'

A daily paper, *Die Wiener Volkszeitung*, carried the sub-title: The Organ of Anti-Semitism.[7]

And yet, historical analysis is apparently no simpler than psychoanalysis. Janick and Toulmin in their *Wittgenstein's Vienna*[8] which was, of course, also Freud's Vienna, suggest that Vienna consisted of several isolated communities which provided highly specific environments with atmospheres all their own. In their view artists, professionals and academics formed a closely knit community who were outsiders not as individuals but as a group and, paraphrasing Schorske, 'not alienated *from*, but rather alienated *with* their whole class'. Now this whole class to which Freud belonged was to a large extent Jewish, and certainly not anti-Semitic. For example, at a time when Jews formed 12% of the population, 48% of the medical faculty were Jews.[7] Within the Viennese intelligentsia which formed Freud's professional reference group, is it reasonable to think of Freud as permanently exposed to anti-Semitism?

On the other hand the story of the delay in Freud's promotion, much discussed by him and others, reveals facts which perhaps put too great a burden on bureaucratic *vis inertiae* as the major explanation. Freud was academically very ambitious. He was given the title Professor in 1902 without ever obtaining a chair at the University, but he had to wait seventeen years for the title while the average period for promotion in the medical faculty was eight years.

What of Freud's statements about his lonely struggle against a world hostile to his ideas in the first decade of psychoanalysis? In many places he was explicit about this, particularly in his voluminous correspondence with Fliess,[9] but most defiantly in the motto he chose for *The Interpretation*: *Flectere si nequeo superos, Acheronta movebo* (If I cannot bend heaven, I shall move hell). It is, of course, possible to interpret this quotation from the *Aeneid* as referring simply to the psychological content of the book in which Freud first demonstrated the power of unconscious motivation. But, as Schorske[10] has pointed out, Freud undoubtedly knew the context in which they were spoken: Juno defying Jupiter. What is equally in favour of understanding the quotation as expressing Freud's defiance of a hostile world is that the socialist Ferdinand Lassalle had used the same quotation on the title page of one of his pamphlets; and Freud was reading Lassalle at the time.

Once again it is Ellenberger who doubts the external reality behind Freud's description of his isolation. In support, he mentions that a number of respectful reviews appeared soon after the publication of *The Interpretation*. Jones,[11] however, refers to one of the reviews so mentioned as 'most stupid and contemptuous'. He also mentions that a university professor at that time lectured on hysteria, concluding with this hardly veiled reference to Freud: 'A colleague in this town has used this circumstance [i.e. that sick people have the inclination to unburden their minds] to construct a theory about this simple fact so that he can fill his pockets adequately'. Jones also tells us that it took eight years to sell the six hundred printed copies of the first edition of *The Interpretation*.

It is easy to see from these few examples that the real world in which Freud lived was multi-faceted and conducive to selective perceptions. It is somewhat less easy to see why his commentators look, as a rule, at only one of these facets. In the case of Jones and Ellenberger the evidence is indeed one-sided. Jones was a disciple; Ellenberger was not only concerned with countering the legend and hero worship that had sprung up around Freud, he also wished to emphasise an idea for which Fechner, Freud, Jung and others served him as examples: profound psychiatric insight, he believes, is as a rule required during a prolonged period of inner turmoil which he terms a creative illness. There is in Freud's explicit admission of his early neurotic symptoms enough material to support this idea. One cannot take issue with Ellenberger when he stresses Freud's selective perception and links it to his neurosis. The pity is only that his concern with the idea of creative illness led him to a somewhat skewed presentation of the world in which Freud lived.

Where, then, does this leave us in the central issue underlying the biographical controversies: is psychoanalysis the idiosyncratic product of a distorted mind, or is it a body of thought which cannot be brushed aside by reference to the troubles of its originator? On the evidence presented so far the case is unproven. Many biographical details remain unclarified and some are unclarifiable. Freud himself wanted his work judged on its merit by criteria independent of his personality. Both Ellenberger and Jones would agree with him and between themselves that psychoanalysis can stand that test. But it would be wrong to ignore the issue, which has a way of intruding itself surreptitiously into more substantive controversies.

First among them is the question of whether psychoanalysis as a therapy works. Freud himself set limits for the therapeutic value of his technique on various occasions in various ways. He thought that psychoanalysis was most suitable for hysterical and obsessional patients who remained in touch with reality, but not suitable for psychotics who had withdrawn from reality and whose pronounced narcissism prevented them from establishing a relationship with the analyst. In general he believed that to profit from his techniques a patient needed a reasonable degree of education, a reasonably reliable character, and should preferably be less than fifty years old.[12] When the symptoms were dangerous he thought that the first task should be to relieve them before undertaking the long and laborious process of psychoanalytic re-education proper.[13] He did not claim a monopoly for psychoanalytic treatment, even when these conditions were met: 'There are many ways and means of practising psychotherapy. All that lead to recovery are good'.[14] Aware of the economically privileged position of most of his patients, he also dreamed of extending his technique to free outpatient clinics where, he thought, the technique would probably have to be modified by including suggestion and hypnosis.[15] He anticipated that this treatment method would be overtaken within half a century by biochemical therapies,[16] and in 'Analysis Terminable and Interminable' he expresses deeply pessimistic views about the possibility of total cures.[17] In a letter to Oskar Pfister he said: '. . . the optimum conditions for [psychoanalysis] exist where it is not needed—i.e. among the healthy.'[18]

From his own casework he reported both, successes and failures, but it is impossible to form an estimate of their balance. Early in his career, when discussing the possible weight of the hereditary component in hysteria, he had confidently claimed that only a major statistical study could ever decide the issue; when Rank later produced the idea of a birth trauma,[19] Freud once again advised caution until empirical evidence became available. But years later, in considering the success of his therapy, he rejected the idea of a statistical check on the grounds that individual cases varied so much on so many variables that comparisons were impossible.[20]

Not surprisingly, contemporary controversies over the effect of treatment of emotional disturbances heeded his earlier and not his later attitude to statistical verification. There is an often quoted article by Eysenck[21] who collated data available at that time on the success of various forms of therapy and arrived at the conclusion that psychoanalytic therapy did somewhat worse than no therapy at all. Given the enormous difficulty in making comparisons of such material, which must be related to the degree of illness at the outset of treatment, the vexed question of diagnosis and the even more troublesome matter of criteria for success of treatment, Bergin[22] has recently taken the trouble of returning to the original data used by Eysenck and gone over his assumptions and arithmetic. This always illuminating procedure yielded the conclusion that psychoanalysis was successful in 95% of the cases at Eysenck's disposal. Now Bergin is careful to point out, first, that he himself is not a psychoanalyst and, second, that his own calculations, while arithmetically correct, should not be taken as more valid than Eysenck's results. All he did in an effort that cannot avoid being based on certain assumptions was to substitute a positive bias for Eysenck's consistent choice in favour of anti-psychoanalytic assumptions.[23]

Psychoanalysts have been stimulated by their own experience and by such attacks on their therapy to investigate their success rate. Recently the results of a monumental evaluation study which began in 1954 at the Menninger clinic were published,[24] and these will undoubtedly form the basis of further research and further controversy. One of the findings —the greatest benefit accrues to those patients who start analysis with a certain amount of ego strength—confirms Freud's hunch when he said analysands should have a reliable character and be relatively healthy.

Research in this area concentrates, of course, on the therapeutic effect of psychoanalytic treatment. This is why one possible impact of psychoanalytic treatment of relevance to its relation to academic psychology, has apparently not yet received systematic attention: its cognitive influence on the minds exposed to it. Particularly in the heyday of psychoanalysis before the Second World War many psychologists sought the experience not only in order to obtain help with personal troubles, but also because they felt a professional curiosity about it.[25] Whether or not these psychologists used psychoanalytic concepts in their future work—some did, others did not—it appears to me that a noticeable and lasting *intellectual* influence occurred. Although it would be rewarding, such a study would face all the difficulties of research in which matters count which cannot be counted.

Freud's relatively pessimistic view of his therapeutic method was bearable for him because even though he said that psychoanalysis was 'born out of medical necessity'[26] he saw its lasting contribution elsewhere as a theory and a research method, 'an impartial instrument, like the infinitesimal calculus, as it were.'[27] He was a reluctant physician. Medicine had not been his first professional choice; he claimed he had not sufficient sadistic impulses to have to sublimate them into the wish to cure others. And yet, so he claimed, he learned all he knew from his patients.

It is this very claim which has given rise to another controversy with curious personal overtones, to put it mildly. David Bakan[28] suggests that Freud's inferences, whether right or wrong, do not stem from clinical observations but are superimposed on them by a fertile imagination nourished in his youth by the study of cabalistic Jewish thought. Freud's ancestors were certainly steeped in the orthodox hasidic traditions, and he had mastered Hebrew in his youth. Bakan leaves it open whether Freud deliberately disguised Talmudic teaching as clinical observation—a sort of reversed Piltdown hoax in psychology—or whether unconscious memory coloured the meaning of his actual or apparent clinical observations. The fact is that he is able to produce some amazing parallels between cabalistic thought and psychoanalytic ideas, particularly with regard to the role of sexuality.

Others are even less reticent in voicing their suspicion about Freud's inferences from clinical data. Frank Cioffi[29] has recently raised the extraordinary question: 'Was Freud a liar?', and answered this sensational headline to his own satisfaction by saying that, while Freud's own account of how he arrived first at the theory that hysteria was the result of a child's early sexual seduction and later of its rejection 'is completely untrue', Freud was, after all, not a liar but 'suffered a massive amnesia' of the facts in this episode. The matter would hardly be worth considering were it not based on the most meticulous textual analysis of Freud's various statements on it, an impressive method which Cioffi had used previously in his attacks on Freud, and which does indeed reveal inconsistencies. Cioffi uses his scholarship to say that Freud was a pseudo-scientist, engaging in the 'habitual and wilful employment of methodologically defective procedures (in a sense of wilful which encompasses refined self-deception).'[30] Indeed, positivists are likely to arrive at similar conclusions, because of their unconcern with the subtle interaction of invention and discovery in creative scientific thought and their assumptions that scientific work is equivalent to operationalism and hypothesis testing.

The claim that Freud was a deliberate obscurantist who was intent on preventing scientists from testing his ideas with established procedures should be confronted with the fact that there exist many hundreds of experimental tests of Freud's hypotheses, some of them proven, others not supported. In the light of this Cioffi should modify his thesis to say that Freud was a bad liar and very clumsy in his efforts to prevent the scientific community from testing his ideas.[31]

If one finds such arguments *ad hominem* obnoxious, it is only fair to add that they were also used by psychoanalysts, indeed by Freud himself,[32] as one of the less attractive features in the debate about the validity of psychoanalysis. Neither the fact that some people resist psychoanalysis for personal reasons of their own nor that Freud may have been influenced in his account of the fate of his seduction theory by complex motives has anything to do with the validity of his thought.

And yet there is inherent in Cioffi's pedantic and arrogant positivisim a controversial point of major importance not only for an appraisal of Freud, but also for an understanding of the dilemmas of modern psychology: the status of psychoanalysis as a science. Is it a science, and if so, what sort of science? Philosophers and epistemologists have joined psychoanalysts and psychologists in a seemingly endless debate on this issue which has already lasted for decades.

Freud himself, who on many other points was ready to emphasise the temporary nature of his formulations which he expected to be modified by others in the light of empirical evidence, was without doubt on this point. 'Psychoanalysis is a natural science—what else could it be?'[33] He was, of course, trained as a natural scientist and had published physiological and neurological research long before he developed psychoanalysis. He held fast to this self-image as a natural scientist and was disturbed, as he says in his early publications with Breuer, that their case studies seemed to lack 'the serious stamp of science'; he grudgingly admitted that they sounded more like fiction.[34]

In his style of thought he was as capable of great leaps of mind as he was of rigorous argument. He argued, for example, on the 'if—then' pattern which forms the logic underlying experiments, that if his hysteric patients suffered indeed from organic lesions as some maintained, then the pattern of their visual, auditory, linguistic or paralytic disturbances should be in accord with known nerve paths. The impediments of his patients, however, did not do so; they suffered as if they had no knowledge of anatomy. Hence, he concluded, the symptoms were psychogenic in origin. He was well aware of the danger of circularity in testing hypotheses from the material that originally led to their establishment; but psychoanalysis was not ready for those tests which carry conviction because they took a different path from that which led to their discovery.[35] It is in that sense that he called himself a conquistador, breaking new ground so that others could examine the scientific validity of his thought. His claim that psychoanalysis was a natural science rests on two pillars of his work: psychological determinism and the psychoanalytic method of observation.

Freud's determinism is of a special kind. First, it is total and unrelenting, much more so than the sense in which some branches of the natural sciences now use it, where the recognition of random factors has led to a weaker form of determinism. In *The Psychopathology of Everyday Life*,[36] for example, while recognising that some parapraxes are determined by mechanical factors, he asserts that the forgetting of lines in a poem which was once known by heart is psychologically determined by the special meaning the forgotten lines carry. Second, the psychologically determining factors can be established retrospectively only, and once discovered cannot be used predictively in other cases. His explanation for what he calls 'this disturbing state of affairs'[36] is rather simple: we cannot yet measure exactly the relative strength of various psychological factors with the result that in circular fashion 'we only say at the end that those which succeeded must have been the stronger'; analysis can recognise causality retrospectively with certainty, whereas prediction is impossible. In all sciences the condition of 'other things being equal' limits their predictive power. Since they never are, neither for the lives of individuals nor for societies, let alone the world, historical prediction, that ancient dream of mankind, turns out to be just another great illusion by which we live but which we must not impose on the scientific study of men or society.

There is a third special feature in Freud's determinism. Psychological events are overdetermined in two ways: the chain of causation can be extended backwards in time. Hysterical symptoms, for example, can be explained by a relatively recent event, but there is one before which determines the power of subsequent events and is, therefore, also an explanation. Overdeterminism refers, secondly, also to the fact that several simultaneous factors, each of them with some explanatory power, contribute to the formation of symptoms.

Freud's second justification for claiming the status of a natural science for psychoanalysis is the psychoanalytic method, which will be discussed in detail in the next chapter. Here it must suffice to indicate the strength of his conviction in this respect by just one statement: 'The poets and philosophers before me discovered the unconscious. What I discovered was the scientific method by which the unconscious can be studied.'

Whether one accepts or rejects Freud's claim about the scientific status of psychoanalysis will depend on several factors; on one's conception of science, on whether or not one distinguishes between natural and other sciences and in what way, and on whether one regards natural science as the most superior way of knowing the world. Freud himself had an exalted and perhaps romantically unrealistic view of science when he said: 'Science is, after all, the most complete renunciation of the pleasure principle of which our mental activity is capable.'[37]

The debate about the scientific standing of psychoanalysis rightly refuses to accept Freud's word for it, but the bitterness of the attack against psychoanalysis as a science remains surprising. One natural scientist wrote recently as follows: 'The opinion is gaining ground that doctrinaire psychoanalytic theory is the most stupendous intellectual confidence trick of the twentieth century and a terminal product as well —something akin to a dinosaur or zeppelin in the history of ideas, a vast structure of radically unsound design and with no posterity.'[38] But the philosopher's debate on the issue is on the whole serious and demonstrates clearly the inherent difficulty of coming to a conclusion. Those who agree with Karl Popper's conception of science that the crucial test of a theory is whether it is falsifiable, and his judgement that in this respect psychoanalysis is pre-scientific,[39] will find much support in the relevant literature. Ernest Nagel in a symposium on psychoanalysis,[40] for example, takes Popper's line in saying that psychoanalysis is not a science, its concepts and formulations are so vague that they cannot be falsified. Yet shortly afterwards he rejects psychoanalysis because some experimental and anthropological data do not support it. He obviously cannot have it both ways. On the same occasion Phillip Frank suggests a conciliatory formulation. He quotes Carnap who distinguishes between logical, semantic and pragmatic components of a theory, recognises the pragmatic value of discovery in psychoanalytic ideas and raises the rhetorical question: why should they not be used for this purpose? This reasonable attitude is actually not opposed to Popper, who recognises that many scientific ideas have their origin in myth. But perhaps this is not a sufficiently discriminating distinction from other sources of inspiration for research. Barbara Wootton, following a similar line of reasoning, quickly concludes that Ibsen, exemplifying some of Freud's theories, 'leaves a sharper impression the mind than the *Introductory Lectures on Psychoanalysis*'.[41] This surely implies a curious underestimation of conceptual formulation. Notwithstanding his early misgivings, Freud was after all not a storyteller but a creator of concepts, struggling for clarity in the difference between concept and entity, particularly with regard to the unconscious. 'Analysts refuse to say what the Unconscious is, but they can indicate the domain of phenomena whose observations has obliged them to assume its existence';[42] and in itself 'the Unconscious is as unknowable as electricity'.[43]

McIntyre, in his book on the Unconscious,[44] begins with the question of scientific status: 'Whether the Unconscious is to be classed with the electron as a notion of great explanatory power or with the ether as a bogus and empty theoretical concept is therefore the crucial question'; he does not answer it in an unambiguous way, but concludes that Freud's chief virtue 'resided in his power to see and to write so that we can see too'. And Wittgenstein, whom he quotes, seems to agree when he says that Freud did not offer explanations—(I take this to mean that psychoanalysis is not a science)—'but a wonderful representation of the facts. It is all excellent similes, for example the comparison of a dream to a rebus.' According to these views Freud was engaged not in explaining but in decoding meaning. The idea of psychoanalysis as hermeneutics has been implied by many, but has been most clearly stated by Habermas.[45] I shall return to this issue at a later stage.

However this may be, McIntyre's concluding phrase implies that there is some truth in what Freud saw. Yet the 'facts' which Freud described so that others could see them too, are in themselves subject to controversy. Nothing, perhaps, created more disbelief, unease, hostility or ridicule already in his own day and even among his supporters than the 'facts' which Freud subsumed under the term of infantile sexuality. Infantile sexuality was first attacked as an offensive word. In 1907, when Jung still belonged to Freud's intimate circle, he pleaded for replacing the word 'sexual', and a year later Bleuler repeated the plea with even greater urgency.[46] Freud remained adamant in terminology and content. Indeed, he often said that the 'facts' of infantile sexuality were so obvious to the naked eye, once they had been stated boldly, that it was a sheer miracle that they had not received full recognition before. There were, of course, some forerunners. Freud himself quoted a medical doctor, Sanford Bell, who in 1902 had collected upwards of 2,500 observations of infantile sexuality, and another, Lindner, who already in 1879 had described thumb-sucking as sexually pleasant. Ellenberger quotes more, and the world literature contains many relevant examples, outstanding amongst them Rousseau's confession of his perverse sexual experience in childhood.

Freud regarded the various manifestations of infantile sexuality as 'facts'. But 'facts' in science are not as straightforward as facts in a telephone directory. They are always established in the light of some hunch, idea or concept from which they derive their importance. Those who doubt Freud's statements about infantile sexuality have thrown doubts on the importance Freud attached to these facts by trying to demonstrate that the inferences Freud drew from them could be disproved. Fact and inference are indeed often difficult to disentangle in Freud's work, and testing the inferences as a way of approaching the factualness of infantile sexuality is, of course, a legitimate procedure. Several empirical psychologists have collected relevant research and commented on it. One of the earliest surveys of research into infantile sexuality[47] concluded that there was no supportive evidence. Another found some support for Freudian concepts, but none for early sexuality.[48] The most recent one,[49] in contrast, discovers studies which, since they support inferences from infantile sexuality, lend support to the underlying 'facts'. Once again, controversy continues.

There are other controversies, serious or trivial, which will emerge in subsequent discussions. Apart from those about Freud's life history, they concern matters which are also controversial in contemporary psychology: the impact of method on the subject matter of investigation; the appropriate level of theory construction; the validity of research results at different times and in different contexts; but above all the peculiar status of psychology as a science: natural science? social science? humanistic science? or outside the scientific enterprise altogether? These issues may be fought about most tenaciously when it comes to psychoanalysis. But one need not look very far to discover that they also plague academic psychology.

CHAPTER 2

From Hypnosis to the Psychoanalytic Method

FREUD's own claim to the scientific status of psychoanalysis rested, as we have seen, on his belief that he had invented an 'impartial' method to explore the human mind below the surface of conscious experiences, that easily available top of the iceberg. What is this method?

In psychological textbooks it has become customary to present theory and problems separately from methods of investigation, so that the latter appear relegated to the status of technical know-how, applicable to a vast variety of research problems. Test construction, attitude measurement, the repertory grid technique, the semantic differential and other techniques are described in our contemporary method-centred psychology as if their inventors had not struggled with substantive problems for which these approaches appeared promising; but they had, at least some of them (Binet, for example, with the practical problem of school organisation; George Kelly with his conception of personality). However important the organisation of technical know-how is for the student of a discipline, the established practice of presentation in textbooks disguises rather than reveals an essential element in creative research: the continuous interplay between assumptions, problems, invention of method, discovery and subsequent modification of method.

In Freud's case a description of the method, by which he set so much store, would be particularly inappropriate without tracing the intellectual history of its development; not only because it took him the best part of twenty years to formulate its essential features, but also because a description without a statement of the theoretical and practical problems

20

which gave rise to its modifications would be meaningless. A historical stance is therefore indicated.

Early in Freud's academic life, when he was much involved with his neurological work and hoped to make his career in that field, economic necessity put an end to that dream. In conversation with his admired teacher, Professor Brücke, the reality principle triumphed over the pleasure principle.[1] Brücke told Freud that it would take many years before he could hope to make a decent living through theoretical research. Freud was at that time much in love with his future wife and wanted to marry and raise a family. The only rational way for him was to enter the practice of medicine. It was this reluctantly taken and at the time frustrating decision which led him to his life's work. He did not realise then that becoming a practising professional with a mind set on theoretical problems and research constitutes a peculiarly favourable atmosphere for breaking new ground.

In the last decades of the nineteenth and in the beginning of the twentieth century the Viennese middle class contained apparently a surprisingly large number of persons with severe neurotic, particularly hysterical symptoms. In Freud's early case studies[2] one finds, for example, a young mother, ostensibly wishing to nurse her baby, but beginning to vomit as soon as the baby was put to the breast; partial paralysis without organic cause; the famous Anna O. who at times had amnesia for her native German, but could speak English. Such dramatic hysterical symptoms are nowadays, interestingly enough, quite rare. At the time of Freud's entry into the clinical field, however, they presented a serious problem to the medical profession. Doctors were divided in their approach to such disturbances. Some took a tough moral line, telling the patients to pull themselves together because there was nothing wrong with them; others used a softer approach from which health spas and sanatoria derived considerable profit, recommending rest cures, taking the waters, a change of scene or some electrical treatment for a paralysed limb. Serious cases were sent to expensive private hospitals, if they could afford it, where they received largely custodial care. An example is the Wolfman, whom Freud later treated,[3] who was sent to such a place by Kraepelin himself. In addition to these medical practices there were in Vienna, and also in Russia according to the Wolfman's memories, but above all in France, efforts to deal with such symptoms by hypnosis. While interest in hypnotism had never completely faded away since the heyday of Mesmer, its later mixture with spiritism had rightly undermined its medical respectability,[4] at least in Vienna. Nevertheless, Breuer, a Viennese general practitioner of high standing, had achieved remarkably successful cures through hypnosis. He had not published them at the time he communicated them personally to the young Freud, who later succeeded in persuading Breuer to a joint publication, the *Studies on Hysteria*.[5]

Freud had acquired his interest in hypnosis in France. In 1885 he had been awarded a travel scholarship for study in Paris. There he became an admiring student of Charcot's; he also familiarised himself with Pierre Janet's work and visited Bernheim and Liébault in Nancy. These men all practised hypnosis and were at the height of their fame. Charcot's lectures and clinical demonstrations impressed not only his students but also fashionable Paris society. Soon after his death, however, he became discredited and ridiculed when it emerged that some of his patients at the Salpetrière could, for a small fee, produce the most astounding symptoms. It is not known whether they were already coached during Charcot's lifetime by his assistants, but this has been asserted. This is an appropriate reminder of a difficulty confronting all who deal with neurosis: the separation of genuine symptoms (genuine in the sense that they are not under voluntary control) from sham or malingering. But whatever the truth in the case of Charcot, Freud's knowledge of hypnosis was not based on him alone. The French practitioners of the art differed from each other in the purposes to which they put hypnosis and in their theories about the origin of neurosis. What excited Freud's theoretical imagination, however, was the phenomenon itself, not its theoretical underpinning, demonstrating once again his profound conviction that immersion into the *explicandum* was the necessary precondition for arriving at explanations, not the other way round as required by the hypothetico-deductive method. Theories can be discarded, observations not, he was to say much later. It is this ability to formulate a theoretical question from a concrete and detailed observation that best describes the bent of his mind.

In the case of the hypnotic demonstrations, the unanswered questions were legion. How could one understand obedience to a post-hypnotic suggestion such as to open an umbrella inside the house, explained by the then fully awake person with the most feeble rationalisation? Or, and most important for the development of psychoanalysis proper, how was one to understand the curious phenomenon that under hypnosis people were able to recapture memories which apparently were not available to them outside hypnosis? Even though Freud abandoned hypnosis completely later on as we shall see, one of the fundamental concepts of psychoanalysis emerged from his struggle to find an answer to these questions posed by hypnosis, the concept of the Unconscious.

As Freud himself emphasised he did not, of course, invent the concept. Many before him, particularly Schopenhauer and Nietzsche, had used it. What is new in Freud is the use he made of the concept for constructing a model of the mind or—to be more accurate—two such models, based on rather different assumptions. While he attempted throughout his life to elaborate the second at the expense of the first, he never quite freed himself from it.

The first was conceived in the language of physiology. At the time at which Freud used hypnotherapy he was still much involved with neurological research; within this framework he sought an understanding of the Unconscious which hypnotic phenomena forced him to assume, in a construction of the nervous system. The considerable effort he must have invested in this only became known posthumously as the *Project for a Scientific Psychology*.[6] The intellectual flavour of the *Project* is perhaps best conveyed in the Newtonian prose in which Freud states its two principal ideas in the opening paragraph:

'1. What distinguishes activity from rest is to be regarded as Q [quantity], subject to the general laws of motion.
2. The neurones are to be taken as the material particles.'[7]

Ernst Kris, in his introduction to the volume in which the *Project* was first published, describes its scope as '. . . a coherent attempt . . . to conceive of all the processes concerned as in the last resort quantitative changes. These processes are not confined merely to perception and memory but include thought, emotional life, psychopathology and normal psychology . . .'[8]

While the *Project* already contains some of the ideas in Freud's later work and certainly already much of the future vocabulary of psychoanalysis, and while it has apparently convinced some physiological psychologists of Freud's importance for their field of work,[9] Freud's own implicit judgement of this first model of the mind should not be ignored: he himself did not see fit to publish it.

His second model of the mind (to be described in detail later) speaks the language of psychology. The Unconscious plays as big a part in the second model as in the first. His later way of thinking about it also goes back to what he learned from hypnosis which demonstrated different states of consciousness, or gaps in full consciousness which can be filled under special circumstances. This impressed him particularly when watching Bernheim as a hypnotist. He reports that Bernheim used to ask his patients when they were out of their hypnotic trance what they remembered about it. The immediate response was vague and lacked concreteness. But Bernheim did not take 'no' for an answer. He told his patients that if they made the effort they would remember, he suggested to them that they really knew what had happened, he commanded that they utter it. And under such deliberate pressure many of them did.[10] This phenomenon led Freud to the idea of the permeability of the Unconscious. What was unconscious could be made conscious.

This seems an almost inevitable conclusion from the hypnotic phenomena which Freud observed. And yet it contains the beginning of a difficulty with Freudian terminology that plagued him in spite of his repeated efforts at clarification, and has preoccupied many of his critics:[11] the reification of concepts. Permeability suggested the idea that the Unconscious was not just an explanatory concept, but a physical entity, just as his later use of the term 'psychical apparatus'[12] was to imply. With regard to the Unconscious, Freud clarified the issue much later in one of his metapsychological papers.[13] There he distinguished three usages of the term 'unconscious': descriptive, dynamic and systematic. The descriptive term applied to the content of the Unconscious: this consists of physiological and instinctive processes which remain always outside human consciousness, even though they affect behaviour and experience; pre-conscious materials which come into consciousness relatively easily; and ideas and representations of past events which had been rejected from consciousness. The dynamic usage of the term applied to inferences which became necessary for the understanding of the experience of conflict in people who could not themselves explain the reason for their sense of unease. A good example of this might be Bruckner, who felt himself under a disturbing compulsion to count the leaves on trees without knowing why. The systematic usage is relevant in the language of theory. In this paper Freud goes out of his way to say that the Unconscious is *not* an anatomical entity.

In any case, Bernheim's cases also raised another question which was to be dealt with later on in Freud's psychological model of the mind and led him to stipulate the prototype of all defence mechanisms, repression: why were these patients so reluctant to reproduce their memories of what happened during hypnosis? Freud, the determinist, had to assume a counteracting force.

Freud practised hypnosis for some time, ordering his patients during their trance to abandon their disturbing symptoms, and many of them did. But his restless mind soon became dissatisfied with the procedure. Of course, the

method had decisive advantages when it succeeded, outstanding amongst them the speed with which it dealt with
symptoms. The woman who was unable to nurse her baby
could do so after Freud had hypnotised her twice. But with
the birth of the next child the symptoms reappeared. What
was more, not every patient could be hypnotised. Those who
were regarded the experience as uncanny. As Freud reported
with some indication of hurt feelings, it did not lead the
patient to appreciate the doctor, who had helped after all,
but rather to avoid him. Another reason for abandoning
hypnosis, however, seems to have been that it bored Freud,
the reluctant physician. It did not help him to understand
the functioning of the mind. 'Hypnosis disguises, psychoanalysis reveals' he was to say later on in his own account of
the development of his technique.[14] It is of interest that, after
Freud's death, some psychoanalysts reverted to hypnosis and
could overcome its disadvantages, even its boredom.[15]

However Freud, in co-operation with Breuer, soon began
to modify the simple procedure of hypnotic commands. A
chance observation in the case of Anna O., who invented the
term 'talking cure', led Breuer to the discovery that the
patient's symptoms were relieved after a hypnotic session if
she had, during the session, expressed strong affect. This
changed the use the two collaborators made of hypnosis. No
longer were they satisfied with post-hypnotic suggestions, but
they began to explore the patient's affect and memories. No
longer, therefore, were cures achieved in a session or two,
instead therapy became a long-drawn-out process. Breuer
termed this the cathartic method. It is the results of this
method which are described in the *Studies on Hysteria*, published at a time when the break between Breuer and Freud
was already imminent.[16] Freud found Breuer increasingly
less receptive to his ideas, particularly to the place he had
begun to assign to sexuality in the aetiology of neurosis.

His discovery of the role that sexuality plays in neurosis was
apparently particularly important to Freud for theoretical
reasons. Sexuality obviously established a link between the
somatic and the mental; for Freud, trained as he was as a

natural scientist, this was crucial. Sexuality bridged the gap between body and mind, between his physiological model and the emerging model of psychological representations.

It is not possible to say what role the break with Breuer played in Freud's final turning away from hypnosis as a therapy. He always acknowledged how much he had learned from him and it. But his growing conviction in the light of his practice that the essence of the hypnotic process was a special relation between the patient and the therapist, brought him to the ultimate frustration with hypnosis and its final abandonment. He termed this relation transference (of which more later), which he quickly recognised as a crucial relation not only in hypnosis but also in other relations between medical doctor and patient, and in teaching situations. The frustration arose because this essential element of hypnosis could not be investigated during hypnosis, he thought.[17] To understand transference he needed the co-operation of a fully awake patient. Remembering Bernheim, he discarded the trance and began to use direct or more subtle pressure to induce the fully conscious patient to reveal his hidden secrets. The couch remained as a left-over from the hypnotic situation. In order to increase the patients' effort at memory, Freud told them by way of a strong suggestion that when he put his hand on their foreheads memories would emerge. And indeed they did.

As a rule the episodes recalled under these conditions were unpleasant, shameful and painful to the patients, but they appeared to be clearly related to the symptoms from which they suffered. The effort to forget—repression—had not been altogether successful. The symptoms were a compromise between full admission to consciousness and successful repression, a quasi-respectable substitute, since the former was worse than being ill and the latter unachievable. If this construction was to make sense, a meaningful link must be assumed to exist between the original event and the nature of the symptoms. For Breuer's cathartic method of abreaction of feeling it was enough that Anna O., for example, recalled under hypnosis that the paralysis of her left arm had started while she nursed her sick father; she had then had an hallucination of a black snake. Breuer was content, because the symptom disappeared after that session. Freud was not. To understand the meaning of symptoms in the light of a patient's private mental world became his major preoccupation.

This change from catharsis to the uncovering of the repressed via the study of meaning marks the true beginning of psychoanalysis. Freud wanted to discover the concrete content of the repressed, make it available to the patient's consciousness so that it could be accepted or rejected in a rational manner. How this was to be achieved still took some time to formulate. But at about that time in the development of the psychoanalytic method an intellectual episode took place which, whatever one makes of it, must have constituted a disturbing experience for Freud: his own discovery that what he had confidently reported in print as the insight derived from his emerging method could not be true. In 1896 he wrote two papers, 'The Aetiology of Hysteria',[18] and 'Further Remarks on the Neuropsychoses of Defence'.[19] The first contains the following statement:

> 'It is true that if infantile sexual activity were an almost universal occurrence, the demonstration of its presence in every case [of hysteria] would carry no weight.'

But he rejected this possibility at the time as a 'gross exaggeration'. The second paper contained the statement that the ultimate cause of hysteria was always the seduction of a child by an adult. Both of these statements Freud was soon to recognise as wrong. It is the manner in which he publicly repudiated them which forms the occasion for Cioffi's extravagance in asking whether Freud was a liar.[20] Freud came to realise that what his patients had reported to him were memories not of actual events but of phantasies and early wishes; he also realised that there did not exist an ultimate cause of hysteria. Many years later he considered the problem that some children who must also have experienced such phantasies did not develop neuroses; then he said that psychoanalysis had no answer to the question: why neurosis?[21] Given Freud's precarious position at the time, the attacks which the seduction theory had produced, and his own undermined confidence in what he was doing, there can be little doubt that the need for renegation was a traumatic experience. The question here, however, is not Freud's morality in reports on the episode, but its impact on the development of his method.

At the time Freud had replaced catharsis by suggestion, and it is in keeping with many anecdotes about Freud's early practice that he suggested not only that memories would come back, but also the content of such possible memories. Cioffi appeals to an ideology of how science is conducted when he comments: 'I am saying of the psychoanalytic investigation of the neuroses: this is not what disinterested enquiry looks like . . .',[22] but one need only read the *Double Helix*,[23] or look at the activities of less brilliant scientists in the defence of their hypotheses, to realise that this is an ideology and not a description of how scientists *de facto* proceed. Freud was not disinterested; he, like many other great men, had a passionate intellect. But in contrast to most other scientists he has left behind a progress report on his works that makes it possible to trace where his passionate intellectual involvement misled him, as in the instances given above, where it permitted him to make leaps of the mind which do not come easily to 'disinterested enquiry', and how he struggled to control his scientific imagination so that it should serve the understanding of the mind rather than mystify; this effort is inherent in his repeated emphases on observation and its dominance over theory, but particularly in the progressive modification of his technique.

Freud learned the lesson of his mistakes. Substantively it led him to realise that memory does not distinguish between reality and phantasy. Methodologically he came to abandon suggestion and direct physical contact with his patients. What he had learned, however, from the period in which he used suggestion by pressure of his hand, he translated into further developments of the psychoanalytic method. He had realised the power of unconscious mental life and that, while it was by definition not spontaneously available to the patient, the patient's mind and his active co-operation was the only available source of making inferences about it. He knew that patients were resistant to revealing details of their real or phantasy life, often involving sexuality, which they had freely discussed under hypnosis. He also knew that the relation between doctor and patient mattered to the progress of his therapy. As he described in *Studies on Hysteria*[24] with full detail, the suggestion technique had occasionally produced full visual recovery of an earlier event, but on other occasions apparently meaningless and isolated words. It was the need to help in the case before him, the practical imperative to press on with the task, that led him not to disregard such apparent failure; he pressed again, and other words emerged, leading in the end to a meaningful recollection. The relation of words and things, about which he was to write later on,[25] emerged as a new speculation or discovery influenced undoubtedly by his pre-psychoanalytic work, *On Aphasia*.[26] As far as the psychoanalytic method was concerned, here is the beginning of the technique of free verbal association. Freud began to conduct his interviews with patients on the couch in terms of these lessons learned during his experiments with earlier techniques. But it was still some time before the basic rule of psychoanalytic therapy was fully formulated.

At that time, and perhaps throughout his life, Freud was not an orthodox Freudian. He saw patients for periods as short as twenty minutes or up to an hour at a time, at varying intervals daily, weekly or with even longer delay, for periods of about three months and often less, sometimes just for a walk in the Prater, as in the case of Gustav Mahler. He apparently took a more active role in these earlier sessions than he was later to stipulate, engaging in intellectual argument and even giving advice on immediate life decisions.[27]

As the number of persons who wanted to become analysed or analysts, or both, increased, it became necessary to formulate the rules of procedure systematically. It was just as well that practical necessity forced the articulation of the treat-

ment method, for the intellectual problems inherent in it—
inherent in any method—were formidable. Freud was fully
aware of them and they preoccupied him to the end of his
life. One of these problems is the question of validity: to
what extent were the data obtained an artefact of the method
used? Within the last decade many psychologists have come
to recognise this as a major unsolved, perhaps never fully
soluble, problem in all their work. Awareness of this problem
led Freud far afield from the analytic situation into searching
for the demonstration of validity elsewhere, as we shall see.
For the time being, the task in hand was to reduce, if not
eliminate, the element of suggestion in his therapy. He recognised that free associations were not really free because the
patient remained under the influence of the analytic
situation.[28]

Another major problem was the extension of the method
beyond the treatment of neurotics, for the theory to which
his clinical practice gave rise was a theory of psychology,
normal and abnormal. In keeping with Freud's implicit conviction that method and theory were always closely inter-
dependent, the approach to this problem was the same as the
approach to the question of validity, as will be demonstrated
later on. Again, for the time being, an interim solution became
available as Freud's ideas on the training of analysts developed.

The insistence on a training analysis provided material
from persons who, while certainly not free from neurosis—
who is?—had at least submitted themselves to the analytic
procedure for motives different from those of patients.
Originally Freud thought that self-analysis, such as he had
reported in *The Interpretation of Dreams*, was something anyone
could do, and had answered the question of how to become
an analyst by saying: analyse your dreams. Freud continued
his own self-analysis to the end of his life, but his doubts
about the possibility of doing so successfully increased. As
Reuben Fine said: 'Where at first it was held that anybody
could do what Freud had done, it was finally concluded that
nobody could.'[29]

Pending the later discussion of other approaches to these

problems, the therapeutic method must now be described. It was finally centred on 'the basic rule': the patient's only obligation during the analytic session was to report without censorship the undirected content which came to his mind, however trivial or embarrassing, offensive or nonsensical he considered this material. The couch, with the analyst sitting behind the patient, had the function of helping relaxation and freedom from the social constraints of facing the analyst. The analyst's aim was to identify repressed material, to bring it to consciousness so that the patient could deal with it rationally. On occasions, the analyst offered 'interpretations' (the elucidation of meaning of a single item of material), or 'constructions' (the combination of meaningful single items into a total configuration of the meaning of an event).

The major device for making this procedure effective was the analysis of the transference between patient and analyst. As their relation developed it began to involve the patient's emotions, love and hate, dependence and rebellion; as the patient relived his past, emotions which had been crucial in relation to his parents and other authority figures surged to the surface and were directed to the analyst. The analyst induces the patient to 'work-through' his transference emotions in searching for parallels in the patient's 'real' life, past or present. So as to avoid a realistic justification for the patient's feelings about the analyst, the latter must remain aloof and preserve a friendly neutrality *vis-à-vis* the patient, avoiding all social contact which could serve as 'here-and-now' justifications for the patient's attitudes towards the analyst, which would make the search for significant parallels in the patient's life outside analysis more difficult.[30] The analyst's own emotions *vis-à-vis* the patient could interfere with the therapy, unless he was in control of them, so that he could deal with his own 'counter-transference' to the patient. Hence the need for a training analysis.[31]

It should be noted that the central function of transference in the therapeutic process emerged only gradually. When Freud first became aware of the phenomenon he too (not only Breuer) regarded it almost as a nuisance, a new symptom which increased the patient's resistance to the analytic process. When he began to realise that in the transference relationship the patient actually *experienced* again early emotional conflicts, felt them and not just remembered them, even though displaced from father or mother to the person of the analyst, he changed his mind. Transference became the basic tool for the therapeutic process, which if appropriately handled, could make the past come alive in the immediacy of the here and now. The feelings of love or hate which the patient develops toward the analyst are neurotic to the extent that they are not justified by the analyst's deliberate emotional neutrality in the relationship. While the analyst needs to use this transference neurosis and in the end resolve it, he must not provoke it through his behaviour. The management of this delicate relationship is the most difficult task for the analyst. Failure in this respect is probably the cause of many unsuccessful or prematurely interrupted analyses.

Underlying the 'basic rule' is Freud's unwavering psychological determinism, first discussed in *The Interpretation of Dreams*,[32] and never abandoned, though conceptualisation and terminology changed. His psychological model of the mind implied a complex hierarchical system of the representations of thoughts and feelings created by experiences, linked to each other in a complex, cross-cutting network. The hierarchical element is not a time-dimension from early childhood to the present, but a hierarchy in terms of availability to consciousness. Any nodal point in that network has determined connections to deeper-lying representations; if one followed these connections one could arrive at other nodal points which had escaped awareness or had been repressed. If two nodal points emerged in free association—in one of Freud's early cases, for example, 'concierge' and 'nightgown' —the pursuance of associations would reveal to consciousness the connection between them. This hierarchy is composed of objects which played a role in the patient's life and associated feelings, and is specific to the individual. This is why psychoanalytic therapy requires the active participation of the patient. His associations, not those of the analyst, indicate the path through the circumvention and complexities of the idiosyncratic network. And yet universalities emerged. The skill of the analyst—and analysis, as Freud said, is an interpretative *art*—lies in knowing when to use his general knowledge and when to follow the patient's individual structure. Many failures and mistakes in therapy are the result of premature generalisations by the analyst.[33] To tell a patient who complains about his inability to concentrate that this is due to his unresolved Oedipal complex is worse than useless.

The basic rule may sound easy enough to follow. Philip Rieff describes its liberating effect in glowing terms: 'By waiving the restrictions of conventional logic and prudery, the therapeutic hour provides the patient with a model refreshment. It puts an end to decorum, providing a private time in which anything may be said . . . an oasis in the desert of reticence in which the patient lives . . . The therapist listens, comprehends, does not condemn . . .'[34] But he also realises, as Freud did, that there is nothing more difficult to obey than the basic rule. The chances are that when it has been mastered and the patient begins to enjoy its exhilarating and liberating potentialities, the analyst will tell him that he no longer needs therapy.

In summary then, psychoanalytic therapy is based on the overriding assumptions of psychological determinism and its concern with the content of the mind, rather than with formal mechanisms such as reinforcement and conditioning, which much of academic psychology emphasises. In the language of computer analogy, the task of the analyst is to start from the output of the computer in order to make inferences about the original input based on partial knowledge of the programme and assumptions about the remainder. The inference on input is in the language of meaningful content.

Karl Bühler[35] recognised the peculiarity of psychoanalysis long ago, when he called Freud a *Stoff-Denker* (a thinker about content). But the distinction between content and mechanism implies only a difference of emphasis, and neither for Freud nor for academic psychology a rigid either-or. This justifies entertaining at least the possibility that the two systems of thought may one day become compatible. Such speculation is further encouraged by much recent self-criticism within academic psychology about the limits of a psychology restricted to formal mechanisms and excluding content, purpose and meaning from its purview.[36] But such reconciliation is certainly not in sight, at least not yet. Foucault[37] for one, though deeply influenced by Freudian thought, is convinced that it is impossible to combine psychoanalysis with scientific psychology. He accepts the necessity to assume the unconscious, but he regards it as the signpost beyond which scientific enquiry cannot proceed. Man, by definition unknowable, must forever escape systematic study, and with it all attempts to understand him in a holistic fashion. He writes: 'It is comforting, however, and a source of profound relief to think that man is only a recent invention, a figure not yet two centuries old, a new wrinkle in our knowledge and that he will disappear again as soon as that knowledge has discovered a new form', abandoned because impossible.

These comments take us beyond considering the development of the psychoanalytic method as a therapy of limited applicability. Freud claims he used it also as a research instrument which yielded rich theoretical harvests. But he was obviously ambivalent about using nothing but therapy for his broader psychological purpose, and restlessly concerned with finding ways and means of demonstrating the validity of psychoanalysis outside the clinical situation. It may have been this ambivalence, or just illness and old age, or his alleged contempt for other scientists which led him to acknowledge in the most perfunctory and condescending fashion a communication about an experimental verification of repression.[38] In any case, as George Klein, the psychoanalytically trained experimentalist, noted: 'Academic psychology has tried off and on . . . to slough off the problems of consciousness and unconsciousness, but the ghosts have lived on. Through the momentum provided by the structural concepts of current psychoanalytic theory and by recent advances in observational techniques, there is a real possibility that the ghosts will become at last corporeal and manageable realities in the experimental laboratory.'[39] The pursuance of Foucault's stance might well lead to the statement that not only psychoanalysis but also psychology as a science will become 'a wrinkle' if, as Klein states, it can no longer avoid confronting the Unconscious. One need not share Foucault's pessimism about the study of man nor abandon Klein's optimism to point to the tremendous difficulties inherent in any effort to combine psychoanalytic thought with the scientific methodology of modern psychology. It becomes, therefore, all the more important to enquire into the manner in which Freud tried to make the transition from the clinical situation to normal psychology.

CHAPTER 3

Dreams, Symbols, Jokes and Slips

THE ambition to create a general psychology stayed with Freud throughout his life, even though he had abandoned the *Project for a Scientific Psychology*, his first effort in that direction. The passionate commitment to psychology that he then felt remained. In 1895 he wrote to Fliess apologising for a delay in their correspondence: 'But the chief reason was this: a man like me cannot live without . . . a consuming passion—in Schiller's words a tyrant. I have found my tyrant . . . psychology; it has always been my distant, beckoning goal . . . [my ambition is] to extract from psychopathology what may be of benefit to normal psychology.'[1] And as late as 1930 in his speech on receipt of the Goethe prize he confirmed this lasting passion in more restrained terms, as became the occasion, when he said that his life-work's goal had been 'to elucidate the human mind'.[2] It is the nature of his work, however, even more than his comments on it, which is the most telling proof of this dominant concern. Unless this is clearly understood it indeed 'remains a mystery why Freud should have treated the process of dreaming so seriously'.[3] He did, because dreams were a bridge to general psychology. In the first paragraph of Freud's preface to the first edition of *The Interpretation of Dreams*[4] he notes the similarity between dreams and neurotic symptoms. Dream interpretation became the 'royal road to the Unconscious' of both patients and others.

The Interpretation of Dreams is, by all standards, a remarkable book. It was the first major psychoanalytic work, and Freud regarded it as his most important book. It is based on well over one thousand interpretations of dreams, and it contains the evidence of Freud's self-analysis in providing almost fifty dreams of his own, analysed and interpreted here as

37

examples of various aspects of dreaming and its interpretation. Even though Freud stopped short of a full analysis of his own dreams this is a unique autobiographical record, for it provides insight into the everyday functioning of mental life that otherwise we know at best of ourselves, never of another person.[5] For present purposes, however, its importance lies in the fact that it contains sometimes in embryonic form, sometimes fully elaborated, virtually all the major psychological concepts of psychoanalysis, even though some of them were to undergo drastic revision later on.

The book itself went into eight editions in German, and several in English, during Freud's lifetime. None of these changed the structure or idea content, but mainly added material and qualified or enlarged footnotes. Freud clarified, expanded and changed some of its statements, however, in other publications.[6] Talcott Parsons considers *The Interpretation of Dreams* 'as one of the great land-marks in the intellectual development of the twentieth century'.[7] The book is organised in seven chapters. The first one of almost 100 pages consists of a review of the scientific literature dealing with the problems of dreams.[8] Chapters 2–6 deal with the psychoanalytic approach to dreams, using several hundred examples. It is this major part of the book which Wittgenstein must have had in mind when he expressed delight in the puzzle-solving aspect of psychoanalysis. Chapter 7, 'The Psychology of the Dream Process', brings a change in tone. Even though it still contains some examples, it is in these hundred pages that Freud tries to explain, and it is here that he speaks most clearly a generalised psychological language.

So much has been written about Freud's dream interpretation that a full exposition here is unnecessary. All I shall try to do is to indicate some of the axiomatic assumptions which Freud made, how his immersion into a phenomenology of dreams led him to a functional terminology (which many of his critical commentators have misconstrued as the creation of homunculi), and his conception of psychological processes, particularly memory and thinking.

At the very beginning of Chapter 1 Freud stipulates two axiomatic assumptions by implication. He says: 'In the pages that follow I shall bring forward proof that there is a psychological technique which makes it possible to interpret dreams and that, if that procedure is employed, every dream reveals itself as a psychical structure which has a meaning and which can be inserted at an assignable point in the mental activities of waking life.'

The search for meaning is here axiomatically assumed as a legitimate goal of psychological enquiry. This is, of course, the extreme opposite of the explicit assumptions of behaviourism which, in its heyday, aimed at a psychology devoid of meaning and restricted to formal processes. Much has happened since those days, and a modern behaviouristic approach apparently finds room even for such a psychoanalytically inspired technique as projective tests.[9] Nonetheless, the issue remains to be faced squarely and openly. In their theoretical pronouncements modern behaviourists insist that the goal of psychology is to identify formal processes, such as reinforcement, which permit one to predict and control behaviour. In practice, for example in behaviour therapy, the search for meaning apparently occurs in the informal preparation of a patient for experimental behaviour modification. Not only is there an effort to establish good rapport with the patient, but his feelings about the symptoms, the occasions of their origin and the circumstances under which they wax or wane are elicited. As we shall see later on, Freud himself also tried a combination of search for meaning with formal processes, even though his main emphasis always remained on the former. That the elucidation of meaning, not just of mechanisms, is the goal of psychoanalysis is a difficult and troublesome axiomatic assumption not only for psychologists but also for modern philosophers of psychology. Cioffi is right when he says about Freud's interpretation: 'everything is what it is *and* another thing',[10] but he is wrong in implying that this disposes of Freud. William James, for one, must have shared Freud's axiomatic assumption. Otherwise his reported opening remark to a Harvard class could not have been made: 'Why is it that a perfectly respectable man may dream that he has intercourse with his grandmother?'[11]

The second implicit axiom is the assumption of unity of personality. Waking life and dreaming are both manifestations of the mental life of an individual, complementary to each other in content, feeling and thinking; the interpretation of one requires the interpretation of the other.[12] Freud never bothered to state this axiom explicitly, but it pervades all his work. He comes nearest to such a formulation in Chapter 7 of *The Interpretation*: 'No conclusions upon the construction and working methods of the mental instrument can be arrived at or at least fully proved from even the most painstaking investigation of dreams or of any other mental function taken *in isolation*' (Freud's italics).[13]

Some commentators, however, have sensed the importance of this axiom. David Rapaport, for example, in one of his early efforts to formalise psychoanalytic theory, emphasised that it eschewed segregation of conation, cognition and affect as much as segregation of memory, association and imagination, and that it combined concern with function and structure.[14] Academic psychology, as far as I know, has never challenged this axiom in a theoretical statement. But neither has it tried to live up to it in research. As a rule it studies either cognition *or* affect, memory *or* imagination. Even so remarkable a psychologist as Piaget has limited his concern to cognitive development, though he has achieved a combination of function and structure. There are, as a rule, very good methodological reasons for these customary segregations. We would probably not know as much as we do *de facto* about thinking, learning, perceiving and remembering, had their study always been pursued with an eye on their interaction. But there is a price to be paid for rigorous methodology: the unity of personality had to be sacrificed to an extent that justifies paraphrasing Krech's and Klein's question: 'where is the perceiver in perception?'[15] to 'where is the person in academic psychology?' It is true we do not yet know, perhaps can never know, how to be rigorous in implementing Freud's concern with all aspects of a person, past and present. But it is also true that many of those psychologists who have studied a highly specific aspect of man feel they have arrived at a dead end.

A third axiomatic assumption in *The Interpretation of Dreams* is explicitly stated: 'We have constructed our theory of dreams on the assumption that the dream-wish which provides the motive power invariably originates from the unconscious—an assumption which, as I myself am ready to admit, cannot be proved to hold generally, though neither can it be disproved.'[16] As a matter of fact one could argue that in one sense this axiom hardly needed stating, for it is true by definition. Since nobody asserts that dreaming is under conscious control, where else could it come from but from that sphere of mental activity outside conscious control which is tantamount to the unconscious. I cannot help thinking that Freud's formulations went wrong in this respect. It is the wish-fulfilling character of the dreams which he axiomatically assumes, not just its origin in the unconscious. The basic function of dreaming, Freud thought, was to protect sleep; in this sense dreams fulfil a conscious wish. Specific dream content, however, fulfils wishes which stem from the unconscious. *The Interpretation of Dreams* is full of examples of Freud's ingenuity in arriving at a dream interpretation in line with this reformulated axiom, some of them exceedingly funny. Freud mentions, for example, the dream of a patient in which she was spending a holiday with her mother-in-law, a thought which she abhorred in waking life. She challenged Freud by saying that this example contradicted the idea that dreams were wish-fulfilments. No, said Freud, what you really wanted was to prove me wrong, and your dream fulfilled that wish. Freud, who could always see a good joke, added, however, that there were in the case more serious matters at stake which further explained the patient's unconscious wish that he should be wrong.[17]

While Freud maintained the idea that every dream had meaning, he did not think that every dream could be interpreted, nor that an interpretation when actually achieved

ever exhausted all possible meanings. He warned psychoanalysts not to engage in dream-interpretation on a *l'art pour
l'art* basis in therapy, but to subordinate it to other require-
ments of the treatment process, and advised them to drop
efforts at interpretation where they did not seem to add to
the analytic procedure.[18]

Freud acknowledges that the idea of dreams as wish-
fulfilments was not original to him. Nobody else, however,
has taken it quite as far as he did. It is, of course, linked to
his more general formulation of the pleasure principle which
governs all unconscious processes, striving after tension
reduction. In the normally functioning individual the
pleasure principle is modified by the need to cope with
reality—the reality principle. These ideas, indeed the whole
of Chapter 7 which contains in more or less detail the beginning of almost all Freud's major theoretical ideas, go of
course far beyond the interpretation of dreams, but they are
invariably linked to the minutest details of dreams and the
psychoanalytic method of trying to understand them. What
is that method?

Its goal is to arrive at a meaningful interpretation, that is
identification of the particular wish underlying the manifest
dream content; this wish is not always sexual but often so.
Some experience during the day before the dream—the day
residue in dream content—has activated a wish or experience not in full consciousness at the time. The psychological
model of the organisation of mental life (described before)
makes this understandable in principle and also indicates the
method for decoding meaning; free association to every
element of the manifest dream content in order to arrive at
the latent dream thought. Some people some of the time, but
small children almost always, dream their wishes straight-
forwardly and do not use the bizarreness of most dreams to
disguise their meaning. In most adults decoding is required
because while in the ultimate privacy of dreaming they can
drop social constraints and rational thought, when they
become consciously aware of their dreams these constraints
are already operating again. Repressed feelings, and ideas

available while dreaming, once again become repressed. Freud suggests—even though there is no way of knowing whether the conscious recall of a dream is identical with the actual dream or already a disguise of its meaning—that in many cases constraints already operate during the dream. He calls this the dream work, i.e. a censorship of the latent dream thought.

Whether one thinks of the censor as operating during the dream or after, the very idea of a censor has induced many to ridicule Freud for introducing a homunculus operating inside the mind and on it. Freud's terminology, even the German habit of capitalising all nouns, may have contributed to this misunderstanding. It requires nothing but a reading of Freud himself rather than of his critics to realise that the censor is only a name for a psychological function, the sifting of content and meaning admitted to full consciousness.

Indeed, academic psychology has many related concepts which could equally be ridiculed or equally admitted to the psychological conceptual armament. Selective perception or perceptual defence are two such concepts; Broadbent's filter theory for memory and perception is another example.[19] The filter has no more physiological reality than the censor. The difference between them is that Freud's functional concept is governed by concern with meaning and content, while Broadbent's is purely formal. What the latter gains in respectability, it loses in explanatory power. All that Broadbent can say is that something is filtered out; Freud is concerned with the what and the why of filtering. It is, however, worth noting that Freud and Broadbent agree that perception is the beginning of all experience.

How does this censorship function operate? Freud identifies four processes which help to disguise the nature of the underlying wish. The first he calls condensation. Dreams are often relatively meagre and compressed, certainly when compared with the result of their interpretation, even though Freud says that interpretation is never complete and could be carried on almost indefinitely. One element singled out for free association connects with several distinct chains of events and dream thoughts; or a person in a dream may bear the name of a colleague but the face of one's brother. Since dreams often treat words as if they were things, words too are condensed into neologisms or psychological puns; a famous example is Freud's dream using the term 'Autodidasker', which analysis revealed to be a conglomeration of 'autodidakt' (self-taught) and the name Lasker, which was associated with Lassalle.[20]

The second censorship process is displacement. The central dream thought often emerges from a minor detail in dream content which apparently has little intensity. Interpretation reveals that the feelings appropriate to the dream thought were displaced on to another element. For example, Freud dreamed affectionately that a friend of his was his uncle. The association revealed that the affection was a displacement, that he regarded his friend as a simpleton who did not deserve the academic promotion which Freud himself so coveted. Displacement often turns feelings into their opposite. This idea of the closeness of opposites is important in Freud's thoughts far beyond the unravelling of the dream work. The closeness of love and hate, or the fact that contrasting con-ditions—say, an overprotective or a rejecting mother—can result in similar impact on the offspring, or similar conditions in vastly different manifestations, is once again a feast for those critics who seek in psychology for 'one-cause—one-effect' relationships. Yet, in academic psychology such com-plexities of human beings become acceptable when they are expressed as U-shaped curves. That authoritarian leadership, as well as absence of leadership, for example, can lead to aggressiveness in children is fairly well established.[21] But reference to statistical curves is certainly not a Freudian-type argument. And it is, of course, true that the nearness of opposites in displacement in dreams and in all psychic life complicates interpretations enormously and leaves room for arbitrariness.

Freud was well aware of this difficulty, but he maintained that the difficulty was inherent in the subject matter, not in the method and concepts of psychoanalysis which only tried to do justice to human complexity. Throughout his working life he was, however, concerned with assembling confirmation of the idea of closeness of opposites. He found it in folk wisdom, in myth and fairy tales (the ugly frog turned into the beautiful prince), in legend and poetry, in primitive ritual, but above all in language with its remnant of primitive thought.[22] He was much intrigued to discover that in ancient Egyptian the word *khen* stood for warm and cold;[23] Japanese has one word for 'Yes' and 'No'; *personne* in French means 'person' but also 'nobody'. Freud noted that the dream interpreters of antiquity made use of the notion that a king in a dream can mean its opposite. Like the examples in ancient vocabulary the dream disregards negation and uses the same visual image to express contrary meaning.

Freud is not the only psychologist to use language for guessing primitive modes of thought. Asch once pointed out that in languages of very different roots character descriptions now understood as complex abstractions from behaviour are based on visual perceptual imagery, such as straight, crooked, all round, etc. The point is relevant because Freud regarded visualisation and dramatisation of thoughts as another characteristic of dream language. This regression to the visual is indeed the third process implied in censorship. That perceptual imagery is earlier and more primitive than rational thought is in line with Piaget's concept of intelligence which he regards as the gradually acquired ability to stand back from information received by sense impressions.

The last process subsumed under censorship is symbolisation. Once again we are on controversial grounds and dealing with a process relevant in dream interpretation and beyond. There is, of course, no controversy about man's power to create and use symbolisation. What is being questioned are two aspects of Freud's thoughts about dream symbols; that they are as a rule employed in dreams to stand for sexual matters, and that they often have a fixed and universal meaning. *De facto*, Freud is fully aware of the fact that these two rules permit of many exceptions and that 'the presence of symbols in dreams not only facilitates their interpretation but also makes it more difficult'[24] because it is hard to tell whether a particular instance follows the rule or is the exception to it. A king can stand for itself or be a sexual symbol. People share symbols but are also able to invent idiosyncratic ones. Popular humour and dirty and not so dirty seaside picture postcards find it less difficult, however, than many an academic mind to accept these two rules. There exists also some indirect experimental evidence to show the operation of the universality of sexual symbolism. Hartmann[25] used the Korsakoff syndrome—a psychotic condition whose most striking symptom is that patients suffer from an impaired ability to retain information—to demonstrate the universal character of sexual symbols. He told patients short stories of crudely sexual content, and found when he subsequently asked them to retell the stories that knife or shotgun, for example, replaced the word penis. He also mentions other similarly confirmatory investigations on the mode of representation of sexual material presented to hypnotised subjects in posthypnotic dream suggestions. Unaided by such later evidence Freud, based on his own work as an interpreter of dreams but, as Ellenberger points out, in line with many dream interpreters before him throughout the centuries,[26] lists in *The Interpretation of Dreams* a large number of universal symbolic representations of male and female sex organs.

As this brief discussion of censorship processes has implied, Freud's effort to decode the meaning of dreams led him inevitably beyond dreams into general psychology; inevitably, because the axiom of the unity of personality forced him to assume that the processes of dreaming were part of the indivisible mental life of man.

Starting with the well known phenomenon that dreams are often available on waking up but then slip away, or that one wakes with part of a dream in mind and a conviction that there was more though it resists efforts at deliberate recall, or that a dream suddenly springs to mind in the middle of the day although it was not remembered on waking up, Freud became involved with the general problem of memory. He designed diagrammatically a model of the 'mental apparatus as a compound instrument, to the components of which we will give the names "agencies"', having warned the reader and himself before that 'I shall carefully avoid the temptation to determine psychical locality in any anatomical fashion. I shall remain upon psychological ground . . .'[27] In spite of such good intentions, however, he is driven back in the course of the discussion to physiological speculations which lead him to define the 'wish' which dreams fulfil in physiological drive-reduction terms.[28]

Virtually like a behaviourist, Freud begins his formal discussion of memory by defining the boundaries of the apparatus thus: 'all our psychical activity starts from stimuli (whether internal or external) and ends in innervations'.[29] Since a stimulus outside the organism cannot be part of the mental apparatus, Freud refers to its representations as perception. Since the function of the perceptual system requires its continuous readiness for the 'here-and-now', a separate but connected memory system (Freud calls it mnemic) must be stipulated to retain information. It is in the several layers of the memory system that associations are formed according to simultaneity, similarity and, one would like to add though Freud does not in this context, meaning. '. . . our memories —not excepting those which are most deeply stamped on our minds—are in themselves unconscious. They can be made conscious; but there can be no doubt that they can produce all their effects while in an unconscious condition. What we describe as our "character" is based on the memory-traces of our impressions; and, moreover, the impressions which have the greatest effect on us—those of our earliest youth—are precisely the ones which scarcely ever become conscious.'[30] Freud goes on to point out the contrast in the sensory quality of memory and perception, and to suggest that consciousness and memory are mutually exclusive. This latter idea is difficult to grasp. For this is either so by definition if memory is unconscious or, to the extent that it can be made conscious, it is wrong by definition. In a later paper, 'A Note Upon the Mystic Writing Pad',[31] Freud suggests that consciousness actually arises instead of memory traces; this and other passages seem to equate consciousness with attention to contemporary stimuli; in this sense incompatibility with memory becomes more understandable to modern ears.

It must be pointed out that many aspects of Freud's model of the mind, and certainly the major part of his terminology, were common intellectual currency just before the turn of the century. There exist a number of books discussing Freud's work in the context of his contemporary climate of thought, outstanding among them Ellenberger's, mostly concerned with tracing the historical origin of ideas in clinical psychology, and Joan Wynn Reeves', mostly concerned with general psychology. It is modern academic psychology which to a large extent has turned away from these fundamental conceptions of the mind because they are outside the range of modern methodology on which psychology's claim to be a science nowadays rests. To give just one example, it is well known that Galton experimented on himself and others with free associations and had this to say about them: 'Perhaps the strangest of the impressions left by these experiments regards the multifariousness of the work done by the mind in a state of half consciousness, and the valid reason they afford for believing in the existence of still deeper strata of mental operations, sunk wholly below the level of consciousness, which may account for such mental phenomena as cannot otherwise be explained.' And, involving memory: 'As I understand it, the subject must have a continued living interest in order to retain an abiding place in the memory. The mind must refer to it frequently, but whether it does so consciously or unconsciously, is not perhaps a matter of much importance.'[32]

This is a language similar to that which Freud spoke, even where there is disagreement; but very different indeed from the language of most psychologists in the 1970's. Only a few psychoanalytically informed experimentalists have tried to tackle such problems of the organisation of the mind with modern methods. Experiments on subliminal perception,[33] for example, bring evidence that not only memory but also perception can function below consciousness; Hilgard's experiments on the experience of pain under hypnosis[34] present another such effort at elucidating various states of consciousness.

There can be no question that Freud's formal model of the mind and the place of memory in it contain ambiguities. Here, as elsewhere, his psychological formulations are more convincing when expressed in the language of purpose and meaning. With regard to memory, the first axiom—the search for meaning—forces him to concentrate on the content of what is remembered or forgotten, so that he can infer from its meaning the unconscious purpose behind the given memory performance. The emphasis on the *unconscious* purpose does not imply disregard for conscious purposes. In conjunction with his clinical work Freud once said that conscious purposes presented no problem because they were fully available to the patient; the unconscious purposes, however, needed a special technique for inferring them. In any case, forgetting is by definition difficult, if not impossible, to achieve consciously. The selectivity of long term memory and the widespread amnesia for events during childhood have not received much attention from academic psychology; they are central evidence for Freud, crucial to his technique, his psychological model of the mind, and virtually all his efforts at explaining psychological phenomena. We shall return to it in the appropriate place.

In one sense it is artificial to separate Freud's thoughts about memory from those about thinking. They are, after all, combined in modern psychology under the term 'cognitive' processes and, what is more, Freud's approach to both topics is very similar. In another sense, however, the separation has the advantage of distinguishing Freud's approach from what is now termed 'cognitive psychology', for Freud cut the cake according to different rules. His thoughts on thinking were based on the axiom of unity of personality and include affect, development, motivation, somatic conditions, clinical conditions, social factors—in fact all the major parts into which psychology has come to divide its unwieldy subject matter for fortuitous historical reasons. It is thinking as an activity of the whole man, not as an isolated function, which is the major characteristic of Freud's approach, once again familiar to his contemporaries and inherent in the ideas of many philosophers before him throughout the centuries. Joan Reeves[35] has analysed the historical and contemporary influences on Freud's ideas about thinking and presented a critical and detailed appraisal of his own contribution—his brilliant insights stemming from his clinical work, his inconsistencies and contradictions. Here it must suffice (in agreement with her conclusions) to single out Freud's major achievement in this area, the distinction between primary and secondary thought processes and his detailed description of the former. In a summary fashion, primary thought processes are strongly influenced by emotion and instinct under the dominance of the pleasure principle, secondary thought processes are modifications of the primary, and dominated by the reality principle. Everybody has, of course, direct conscious experience of both thought processes. Letting one's mind wander encourages primary process thought: images appear, stories are spun, wishes fulfilled, obstacles of time and space and countervailing interests of one's own or others ignored, heroic or criminal deeds performed in phantasy. But then the telephone rings or the family needs a meal and reality testing gains the upper hand.

However, just as during a period of primary process dominance condensed or symbolised images can be quite rationally manipulated, so a secondary thought process may be carried out under the emotional or instinctual halo of preceding or concomitant primary process thought. Freud assumed that thinking in the infant begins with hallucinating the thing which provided pleasure but is now absent, say, the nipple. For a while hallucination satisfies. But not for long, and gradually the baby learns the difference between hallucinated, i.e. primary process, satisfaction and the real thing. As the infant develops, the constraints as much as the possibilities of the real world begin to be appreciated, and secondary thought processes emerge which renounce the immediate gratification of the primary hallucination for the delayed gratification which may result from following the rules of the world, first in action, then in thought. The two processes develop sequentially, but they are, of course, not mutually exclusive. As Hartmann said, '. . . the picture of a totally rational human being is a caricature; it certainly does not represent the highest degree of adaptation accessible to man.'[36]

While Freud developed much of this in later years, *The Interpretation of Dreams* contains the first basic and detailed description of primary processes which the dreamwork employs in its peculiar primary process language; the effort to decode this semantic language led to the identification of its grammatical rules, the censorship processes.

All this—and much more—is presented in Chapter 7 within a complex theoretical superstructure with physiological overtones involving Freud's energy model and the concept 'cathexis' (a term which might have found an easier acceptance in psychology had the otherwise so excellent translator rendered the German word *Besetzung* in a less formidable way, such as, e.g. 'investment'). Later on I shall return to this theoretical model, which involves the various levels of explanation with which Freud struggled. Here it must suffice to say that the identification and description of the two types of thought process stand on their own feet as a major achievement.[37]

Ellenberger summarises his appraisal of the *Interpretation* by crediting Freud with four innovations:[38] 'The first is his model of the dream with its distinction of manifest and latent content and its specific pattern of being lived simultaneously in the present and the remote past. The second is Freud's contention that the manifest content is a distortion of the latent content, resulting from repression by the censor.' This point is equivalent to the distinction between primary and secondary thought processes. But to continue with Ellenberger: '. . . Freud's third innovation was the application of free association as a method for the analysis of dreams, and the fourth was the introduction of systematic dream interpretation as a tool of psychotherapy.'

I would like to add to this list two further items. First, the record of Freud's self-analysis in the book, which certainly qualifies as an innovation. Freud says he used many of his own dreams for the sake of convenience. Here he himself could decide what was a tolerable level of indiscretion. But the self-analysis is important beyond this and its obvious biographical interest. It stakes the claim for psychoanalysis to be a reflexive psychology, that is one capable of turning back on itself, of including the act of being a psychologist in its scope. Second (and this is perhaps only an elaboration of Ellenberger's third point), the *Interpretation* contains Freud's most general psychological and physiological models of the mind together with an effort at their theoretical integration, which far transcends his concern with dreams.

In the *Interpretation* there are, indeed, already casual references to the type of phenomena to which Freud was to apply his psychological theories almost immediately afterwards: slips and jokes, both once again familiar to normal life and hence confirmation for Freud that the theories, concept and ideas which he first developed in the study of neurosis were the basis for a general psychology.

The Psychopathology of Everyday Life appeared in 1901,[39] *Jokes and Their Relation to the Unconscious*[40] in 1905, but both themes had interested Freud for years, and played a role in his self-analysis. *The Psychopathology* went through many editions, each adding many examples of parapraxis, so that the book is now rather overloaded with concrete instances of forgetting names, words, intentions, misplacing objects, slips of the tongue or pen, or apparently unintended actions. They happen so often in everyday life and are, as a rule, so readily understood by the perpetrator and his audience as revealing hidden purposes that the phenomenon of parapraxis can here be taken for granted.[41] Freud manages to demonstrate that they are an inadvertent breakthrough of unconscious repressed ideas using the processes of condensation, displacement, inversion of meaning, dramatisation and symbolisation. The *Jokes* book, which in the original German makes hilarious reading but which is, in its examples, often untranslatable, makes the same basic point: the difference to parapraxis being that one deals here with a deliberate utilisation of primary thought processes in order to obtain and give pleasure.

However, there is in *The Psychopathology* one example which must be singled out for critical examination. It is Freud's relentless belief in the total absence of chance in human actions, his conviction that unless there was a conscious purpose an unconscious one must be assumed, which presents the problem.

Freud refers to a letter he had written to his friend Fliess in which he said he expected the proof of *The Interpretation of Dreams* to contain 2467 printing errors:

'All I meant was some very big figure, but I put down that particular one. However, nothing that happens in the mind is arbitrary or undetermined. You will there-fore rightly conclude that the unconscious hastened to determine the figure the choice of which had been left open by the conscious. Now, immediately beforehand I had read in the newspaper that General E.M. had re-tired as Master of the Ordnance. I should explain that I am interested in the man. While I was serving as a medical officer cadet he came to the sick quarters one day (he was then a colonel) and said to the medical officer: "You must cure me in a week, because I have some work to do for which the emperor is waiting." After that episode I took it upon myself to follow his career, and behold! now he has reached the end of it . . . I worked out how long he had taken over this. As-suming that it was in 1882 that I saw him in the hospital, it must have been seventeen years. I told my wife this and she remarked: "You ought to have retired too!" "Heaven forbid!" I exclaimed. Immediately after this conversation I sat down to write to you. But the earlier train of thought went on in my mind, and with good reason. I had miscalculated; I have a fixed point in my memory to prove it. I celebrated my majority, i.e. my twenty fourth birthday, under military arrest (having

53

been absent without leave). That was in 1880, or nineteen years ago. That gives you one half of the figures in 2467. Now take my present age—43—add 24 and you have 67. In other words, my answer to the question whether I should have liked to retire myself was to say that I should like another twenty-four years' work first. On the one hand, I am obviously annoyed at having failed to get very far myself during the period during which I have followed Colonel M's career, while on the other I celebrate a kind of triumph that his career is now over, while I still have everything in front of me. So one can say with justice that not even the casually scribbled figure of 2467 was without its determination by the unconscious.'[42]

What stance is one to take *vis-à-vis* this episode and its interpretation? It has a flavour of number mystique which, however appropriate in a letter to Fliess who was much given to such speculations, seems to credit the unconscious with mathematical abilities, which are at least at first glance, almost unbelievable. There is no doubt that Freud intentionally searched for meaning in the number 2467. His associations are factual and plausible. The dilemma arises over the question whether the meaning was superimposed after the event on a random number by an extraordinarily skilful mind or whether it was determined in its meaning before interpretation and only required the application of the psychoanalytic method to unravel the unconscious processes. In other words, were the associations 'free' or did Freud, in order to prove the power of the unconscious, first deliberately and consciously play around with the numbers, adding his age to the first two on a trial and error basis, to see what he could construct? Does it matter whether meaning was first supplied by unconscious processes or later superimposed by a successful 'effort after meaning',[43] given that the distinction is so very difficult to make and that the elucidation of meaning provides obvious satisfaction, never mind where the process originated?

It does matter for two reasons. First, because the question preoccupied Freud at various stages of his life. Already in the *Studies on Hysteria* Freud raised the question and left it open:

'Even when everything is finished and the patients have been overborne by the force of logic and have been convinced by the therapeutic effect accompanying the emergence of precisely these ideas—when, I say, the patients themselves accept the fact that they thought this or that, they often add: "But I can't *remember* having thought it." It is easy to come to terms with them by telling them that the thoughts were *unconscious*. But how is this state of affairs to be fitted into our own psychological views? Are we to disregard this withholding of recognition on the part of the patients, when, now that the work is finished, there is no longer any motive for their doing so? Or are we to suppose that we are really dealing with thoughts which never came about, which merely had a *possibility* of existing so that the treatment would lie in the accomplishment of a psychical act which did not take place at the time?'[44]

Was the meaning of 2467 arrived at by 'a psychical act' which took place long after the number had been written down? We shall return to similar doubts in Freud's mind later on. Critics have tried to trap Freud in inconsistency by quoting him out of context. Referring to examples similar to the number interpretation from *The Psychopathology*, they confront this with Freud's statement that 'in the unconscious NO does not exist and there is no distinction between contraries'.[45] The quote is correct, but Freud is here describing the *nucleus* of the unconscious which contains representations of instinctual factors.

In the same paper he goes on to describe various layers of unconscious processes; repressed ideas, which in contrast to the nucleus were once conscious, are described as highly organised, free from self-contradiction, have made use of the acquisitions of conscious life and have features which make them resemble conscious thought, the one distinction being that they are not available for conscious self-reflection without some such effort as Freud put into making sense out of the number 2467. I do not wish to deny inconsistencies in Freud's formulations; there are plenty. But not in the particular case: his theory of unconscious processes encompasses the possibility of both, a-logical and logical operations, just as the primary processes imply. Many, though by no means all, of the apparent contradictions in Freud are due to the fact that the unwary reader (or, dare one say, the unconsciously motivated reader?) has not taken a long enough breath for absorbing his exposition. His line of thought is never limited to a paragraph or even a chapter. Later parts contain qualifications which have to be taken into account for a full understanding of the whole.

But the second reason goes beyond the wish to understand the particular episode or the intellectual struggles and uncertainties in Freud's mind to the substance of the matter: is there any other evidence for the statement that unconscious processes can perform logically complex operations?

Galton's conviction about powerful unconscious layers of the mind has already been mentioned. The most astounding examples, however, of the role of unconscious processes in mathematical inventions have been collected by Hadamard.[45] Even though his material is anecdotal and unsystematic the mathematicians from and about whom he collected the story of their inventions were certainly free from contamination by psychoanalytic thought (several lived before Freud); they had no axe to grind; and the integrity of their self-reports is beyond doubt. Perhaps it is enough to recall here one or two examples. There is the well-known account of Poincaré who, with the intention of dismissing mathematics from his mind for a while, went for a trip into the country: 'Just as I put my foot on the step . . . the idea came to me . . . that the transformations I had used to define Fuchsian functions were identical with those of non-Euclidean geometry.' Or Gauss, who reports that he had been plagued for years with a problem he could not solve: 'finally two days ago I succeeded . . . like a sudden flash of lightning the riddle happened to be solved. I cannot myself say what was the conducting thread which connected what I previously knew with what made my success possible.' As far as I know no other existing psychological explanation does justice to these and other reported phenomena than Galton's or Freud's assumption of powerful unconscious mental processes, capable of logical thought and more.

As for the number 2467, it is possible that Freud's zeal to demonstrate the power of unconscious determination led him to a construction imposed and not discovered. It is also possible to maintain that his unconscious, like that of Poincaré and Gauss, was superior to his conscious mind in putting two and two together. But that second way of understanding how Freud arrived at the number—by unconscious intention rather than haphazardly—remains not totally convincing. It could be argued that the analogy with Poincaré and Gauss should not be stretched too far, for the product of their unconscious was undoubtedly well prepared through many hours of conscious thought, while Freud's number associations do not suggest that he spent much time consciously in adding his current age to that on some previous occasion.

The minor dilemma of choosing between the two ways of understanding this episode reflects the major dilemma about the scientific status of psychoanalysis, and perhaps also about those significant aspects of academic psychology which are inevitably concerned with elucidating meaning. If meaning is inferred from mechanism—which may be conscious or unconscious—there is at least an affinity to natural science. If meaning is imposed to suit idiosyncratic circumstances with disregard for mechanisms—for example in forcing Freud to make clear to himself some of his unconscious preoccupations at the time—it has the power to increase insight; it functions as a heuristic, as an imperative for self-examination which could also have been mobilised by other numbers is unquestioned, but it is then clearly not a natural science. Quite apart from the specific episode, the challenge of Freud's thoughts to psychology lies in his effort to do both, to infer and impose meaning. Freud's construction of the primal horde and patricide in *Group Psychology and the Analysis of the Ego*,[47] which he himself recognised, of course, as a construction, that is as an imposition of meaning, has all the power of a myth and the advantage of fitting with the inferences he made from his clinical observations. But since it is by definition impossible to obtain evidence for these assumed prehistoric events, they are outside the scientific enterprise.

CHAPTER 4

Personality

THERE is, perhaps, no other aspect of Freud's psychology quite as well known in its terminology, and quite as much distorted in popular knowledge and in casual technical references, as his concept of personality. There are several reasons for this. First, Freud had two conceptions of personality, and even though he encompassed the earlier in the later one explicitly, their relation to each other is certainly not simple, and often ignored. Secondly, the terminology which he acknowledged as not being original to him invites a confusion between entity and concept. He was, of course, talking of concepts. What is more, in this context the term 'metapsychology' is used in a rather idiosyncratic way and therefore, not surprisingly, often misunderstood. It does not mean what metaphysics means in relation to physics; metapsychology in Freud's terminology is 'a term that signifies not (as it might seem) that which is beyond psychology altogether, but simply those psychological investigations that are not limited to conscious phenomena, and that formulate the most general assumptions of analysis on the most abstract level of theory.'[1]

Freud's earlier conception of personality he termed topographical, that is viewed on a dimension of depth in psychological space; he distinguishes three 'locations' of mental life —the unconscious, pre-conscious and conscious—which shade into each other, sometimes spontaneously and without difficulty; as a rule, however, distorted by the censorship processes which operate between the unconscious and the pre-conscious, the pre-conscious and the conscious. Transition in the other direction occurs via the mechanism of ordinary memory storage from conscious to pre-conscious or via repression from consciousness to the unconscious. Much of this was, of course, already central to Freud's thought from the *Studies on Hysteria* onwards, even if not identified as a view of the whole person. For decades Freud was too preoccupied with the exploration of unconscious processes to pay much attention to the person as a whole; consciousness appears, as it were, as an afterthought in his earlier writings. Secondary process thinking, a major preoccupation of academic cognitive psychologists, is for example hardly elaborated. There are now some psychoanalysts, outstanding amongst them the Frenchman Lacan,[2] who disregard Freud's later view on personality, reject the development of psychoanalytic ego psychology, and concentrate entirely on his earlier conception; this has led to some fierce hostilities within the psychoanalytic camp. Freud himself never fully redressed the balance between attention to conscious and unconscious processes, even though his second conception of personality pointed the way to it.

This second approach has as its conceptual mainstay that other well known triplet of concepts, Ego, Id and Superego. Psychoanalysts call this the structural approach, implying a conception of structure such as Bertalanffy had in mind when he said that structures were slow processes of long duration, while functions were quick processes of short duration.[3] We are dealing, then, in the second conception of personality with the results of gradual development. Freud's own presentation in *The Ego and the Id*[4] is complex and contains much more than the elucidation of the three basic concepts. In a sense it is, once again, an effort to link together all his theoretical ideas; once again not totally successful and hence an additional reason for misunderstanding or rejection. Karl Popper's remark that the Ego, Id and Superego have no stronger claim to scientific status than Homer's collected stories from Olympus,[5] or Joan Reeves' view that 'Freud's general model of motivation, and that popular triumvirate the Id, Ego and Superego, may strike a still later generation as historical oddities'[6] are examples of the reception of these complex ideas by critics who are certainly not hostile in principle. Neither of them spells out, however whether they object to the conception of personality or the energy theory which pervades *The Ego and the Id*, or the relation of the first to the second view, or the danger of reification of psychic agencies.

Keeping such criticisms in mind makes it important to trace the manner in which Freud arrived at these concepts, which may help to clarify their status. It is much more than a 'myth'.

Even though Freud concentrated for so long on ways of inferring unconscious processes through decoding of conscious material, his habitual attention to minute details in his patients' utterances forced him to recognise different functions of the conscious ego, a term then in common parlance. In particular he was struck by the fact that a subject can regard himself as an object; that is a person can take a critical stance *vis-à-vis* himself, evaluating, praising or blaming. Two types of clinical observation led him to regard this particular split in ego functions as important: first, the significance of this critical function in depressed and melancholic patients where all other ego functions were impaired by an overriding and irrational sense of guilt and worthlessness. Second, he came to realise that this function developed later than other ego processes; small children acquired it only gradually in response to their maturation and to socialising influences from their parents. Taken jointly these two observations seemed to suggest that the ability of the ego to comment on itself deserved a special name. Freud first called it ego-ideal, then super-ego. Now the fact that people can, and do as a rule, form judgements about themselves as objects can hardly be disputed, nor that this self-critical faculty deserves a name of its own. On one level then the super-ego is a descriptive concept on a high level of abstraction for a specific area of mental life. It is well worth pursuing the other two concepts on the same level, as Freud himself did. But before entering into a description of the various functions subsumed under the name of the three psychic agencies, it is appropriate to point out some general features of Freud's mature view of personality.

The first thing to note is that he is never concerned with a static situation, always involved in thinking about processes. In this respect he differs from trait theories of personality, but is similar to other academic personality theories, e.g. Gordon Allport's,[7] in spite of other differences between the two, or George Kelly's personal construct theory.[8] Freud's is a structural–functional conception.

The next general property is Freud's assumption that personality is the result of a continuous interplay between the demands of the organism and external reality. In that respect there is a similarity between his thought and Piaget's concepts of accommodation and assimilation, but a sharp contrast to behaviourism or to Eysenck's fundamentally biologically oriented extraversion–introversion theory of personality. In modern terminology Freud was clearly an interactionist. But the difference to Piaget lies in Freud's axiom of the unity of personality that embraces cognitive, conative and affective aspects. Since Piaget dealt only with cognition, he has of course nothing to say on personality proper.

The next general aspect of Freud's ideas on personality, however, unites him again with Piaget's approach while separating his ideas sharply from those of many other academic personality psychologists: his concern with real time and psychological time. Not only did he engage in a retrospective psychology, but the difficult concept of time entered, as we shall see, into his description of psychological functioning. The difficulty was certainly familiar to St. Augustine who devoted much effort of his brilliant mind to a search for a definition of 'real time', that is external time, only to conclude in defeat: 'For so it is, Oh Lord, my God, I measure it; but what it is that I measure, I do not know.' And yet he did know something of great importance for understanding time perspective in psychology when he left the search for an objective definition and dealt with the experience of time; in this context he spoke of time as a three-fold present: a present of things past but remembered now, a present of things present and experienced now, a present of things future but anticipated now.[9] One can only regret that apparently Freud had not read Augustine's *Confessions*; it might have helped him in formulating his idea of a causality which can be identified only retrospectively and safeguarded him against the accusation of teleology.

These general characteristics of Freud's view of personality form the background against which his description of the three structural–functional psychic agencies must be seen.

The id is a summary term comprising various functions, such as instinctual drives—hunger, thirst, sexuality—which mobilise the whole person and thus have overt consequences. These consequences are behavioural not just physiological, but the instinctual drives are, of course, 'open to the somatic' in Freud's terminology. There are also other functions subsumed in the id which, similarly, have mobilising consequences but stem from previous experiences which became repressed; that is, there are memories of ideas, events, actions and feelings excluded from consciousness but activating the person. These activating functions operate without logical organisation, 'contrary impulses exist side by side, without cancelling each other out or diminishing each other . . . There is nothing in the id that could be compared with negation; and we perceive with surprise an exception to the philosophical theorem that space and time are necessary forms of our mental acts. There is nothing in the id that corresponds to the idea of time; there is no recognition of the passage of time, and—a thing that is most remarkable and awaits consideration in philosophical thought—no alteration in its mental processes is produced by the passage of time. Wishful impulses which have never passed beyond the id, but impressions too, which have been sunk into the id by repression, are virtually immortal; after the passage of decades they behave as though they had just occurred.'[10]

Several things are to be noted about this passage. I have deliberately omitted Freud's reference to energy concepts with which I shall deal in another context, and yet this omission does not impede understanding of the id functions. They can be viewed on a descriptive level only, albeit on a very high level of abstraction. On a slightly less abstract level, the id functions refer to those aspects of human feelings and behaviour which we experience passively, as it were, of whose causes we are ignorant or which we cannot deliberately control. The consequences of these functions do intrude into consciousness as they drive us into actions, into feeling depressed or elated, attracted to one rather than another sexual object, or result in ideas, dreams, thoughts and phantasies; their origins, however, escape conscious introspection. Good common sense psychology and Freud, the determinist, assume that there are causes for such psychological events in the biological and experiential history of a person, but that the gaps in consciousness of our own history prevent us from seeing why we became as we are.

That these events, some never consciously represented, others forgotten or repressed, should have consequences in the here and now defies the willingness of many psychologists to go along with Freud. Consider the ridicule that has, for example, been heaped upon his statement that an early anal fixation may influence the adult character in the direction of orderliness, parsimony and obstinacy.[11] Leaving aside the question whether this is an invariable causal chain[12]—Freud did not claim it, otherwise he would have predicted rather than postdicted,—the ridicule evaporates if it is realised that Freud was using Augustine's subjective concept of time which makes the past that which is present now, and not the objective past time which may have left no trace. The past can be effective now only to the extent that at the time of the original event it produced a modification which persisted in its original form or underwent further changes up to the present. Without this assumption the impact of the past would be on a level with a primitive teleological belief that the future which has not yet occurred influences the present.

Undoubtedly, many psychologists will be more persuaded by Penfield's observations than by these arguments. Penfield, while operating on patients suffering from temporal lobe epilepsy noted that the conscious patients, under local anesthesia only, reported flashbacks to their past, a vivid reliving of previous experience, not just a memory, when the electrode touched the temporal lobe.[13] But the conviction so achieved implies being right for the wrong reason. Penfield's observations are fascinating in their own right as an indication of the essential unity of mind and body, not as a direction to reduce psychology to physiology so as to make it more respectable. The greatest conceivable achievements of physiology in the future will not dispense with the need for a psychological level of discourse which assigns psychological meaning to the impact of the past.

The timelessness, the 'virtual immortality' of unconscious processes refers, then, to aspects of the past which had an impact then and are still operating now. Other past events which did not produce an impact then are, of course, gone for good. The coexistence of contradictions, the absence of negation and of logical organisations in unconscious processes must be understood in a similar fashion, as was already indicated in the discussion of primary processes. The contradictions in the id consist of the simultaneous residue of logically incompatible propositions; each proposition in itself can be perfectly reasonable and rational. A little boy, for example, may at one time wish to be like his mother, that is soft and gentle; at another time like his father, that is strong and aggressive. If both wishes are repressed there may be mobilising id functions in the adult man which are illogical only in their combination. It is the *organisation* of unconscious processes in their totality which is free from those logical constraints where, when one premise negates the other, one of them has to be abandoned; within any element of repressed experience the logic which existed in the once conscious thought continues to operate. Admittedly Freud was not very clear in his summary description on these matters. But the point to be made here is that they can be read as acceptable descriptions of one part of mental functioning.

On the same level, again omitting references to Freud's energy concept, the ego functions can be understood. For in addition to what we are made to feel, think and do by id processes, we also conduct deliberate transactions with the real world in which we live, i.e. we engage in ego functions. Outstanding among these processes is, of course, perception and proprioception, the acquisition of information about the world around us and about our own bodies which give rise to the experience of consciousness. Memory, learning, secondary thought processes and reality-testing, that is the search for a correspondence between internal representations of the world and the behaviour of that world, together with control of motor activities, are dominant features of ego functions. All these processes and activities are, in sharp contrast to id functions, unified and organised. 'The ego stands for reason and good sense while the id stands for the untamed passions.'[14] But though it is reasonable for systematic thinking about personality to distinguish ego processes from id processes they occur, of course, simultaneously so that the ego functions include the channelling and control of id impulses which surge into consciousness and have the characteristics of a demand which cannot be ignored.

In describing the ego functions Freud uses a vivid but misleading anthropomorphic terminology, which makes it easy to accuse him of reification and of Ryle's 'ghost in the machine'[15] when he says 'the poor ego . . . serves three severe masters and does what it can to bring their claims and demands into harmony with one another. These claims are always divergent and often seem incompatible. No wonder that the ego often fails in its task. Its three tyrannical masters are the external world, the super-ego and the id.'[16]

One result of the control function of ego processes is the experience of anxiety; another the development of strategies to deal with life's difficulties, whether they come from inside or outside. These strategies are the defence mechanisms which Freud regards as part of the ego functions. The term 'mechanism' is unfortunate here; they are clearly purposeful strategies, consciously or unconsciously designed to make life easier and more manageable, not mechanical routines with causes but no purposes. Repression is in Freud's thinking the dominating defence. But other strategies such as projection, denial, rationalisation, sublimation and so on also come into play depending on factors and circumstances which Freud spelled out only partially. They are employed not only in illness but also in health in support of the overall synthesising function of the ego in dealing with internal or external conflicts. In this respect defence strategies have a similarity of function with the resolution of cognitive dissonance[17] and with Bartlett's concept of 'effort after meaning'.[18] Neither Festinger nor Bartlett felt it necessary to specify whether these strategies were consciously or unconsciously employed. Concern with degrees of consciousness were then, and are now, largely outside the interests of academic psychology. For Freud it was a dominant consideration and he noted from work with his patients that they were not conscious of these ego defence strategies, which had implications for the combination of both personality theories.

The third group of functions, originally termed ego-ideal, came to be known as the super-ego. Its origin from the oedipal complex will be discussed later and is indeed not necessary for a description of the relevant processes. In any case, it is often ignored that Freud saw the super-ego functions as continuously developing, and not as fully established in early childhood: 'In the course of development the super-ego also takes on the influences of those who have stepped into the place of parents—educators, teachers, people chosen as ideal models. Normally it departs more and more from the original parental figures; it becomes, so to say, more impersonal.'[19] Yet, as the argument develops, Freud retreats from the developmental conception of super-ego functions; discussing parental influences in later years when the child's belief in the omnipotence and magnificence of his parents has been tempered by realistic judgement he writes: 'Identifications then come about with these later parents as well, and indeed they regularly make important contributions to the formation of character; but in that case they only affect the ego, they no longer influence the super-ego, which has been determined by the earliest parental images.'[20] It should be noted that Freud understands by super-ego functions more than the tendency to self-punishment or self-criticism; in addition to this representation of conscience there is also the function of self-observation and the establishment of the ego-ideal.

On this descriptive level, then, Freud has created in this second personality theory not homunculi but a conception on a high level of abstraction of man's transactions in conducting the business of living. Freud meant the three major groups of functions to be comprehensive. Some confirmation that they are central in viewing personality as a whole comes, perhaps surprisingly, from a factor-analytical study. Pawlick and Cattell[21] subjected a large battery of 'objective' personality variables to third-order factor analysis. They conclude as follows: 'Although we did not start our studies with any predilections for psychoanalytic theory, it is a striking fact that the psychoanalytic descriptions of ego, id and superego would fit very well the three major patterns found in this research.'

Such confirmation carries weight precisely because it stems from a totally different point of view and is obtained by independent methods. On the other hand it is, of course, true that one obtains from factor analysis only what was put into the tests used. While the result therefore confirms that id, ego and super-ego are certainly not figments of Freud's imagination, it cannot be used as evidence for the exhaustiveness of Freud's view of personality conceptualisation. Yet the exhaustiveness of Freud's view of personality has never been doubted, as far as I know, perhaps largely because his anthropomorphic and physiological language in discussing ego, id and super-ego have given so much occasion for attack that his classificatory achievement remained hidden. Omitting these interfering modes of discourse, Freud proposes that personality should be regarded as a habitual mixture of purposes to which human actions are geared: satisfying needs of the organism, meeting internalised standards, and relating to the external world, its demands and opportunities.

Here, then, is what Basch[22] calls a classificatory theory of personality, on a level with Linnaeus' botanical classification, arrived at via an abstraction from observations and like every other theory guided by a view of what matters in the phenomenon. Academic psychology, because it achieved independent scientific status at a time when the natural sciences had advanced to explanatory theories, sometimes tried to skip the Linnaean phase of bringing system and order into the phenomena it investigated. Freud shared the ambition for natural science type theories. But he was by professional necessity too meticulous an observer to ignore the raw data in front of him, which showed people at cross-purposes with themselves and the world around them. What the clinical situation revealed were not energy models but strivings and frustrations, from which he abstracted the three major groups of purposes represented by ego, id and super-ego.

A classification of this kind is important to the extent that it provides more than just the satisfaction of orderliness and points the way for further thought and search. The uses to which Freud put his classification are various. Putting aside, once again, physiological speculations as well as the formulation of developmental hypotheses, in the context of personality it is the clinical uses which must be specified: first, the classification of functions is an indicator for describing personality and personality disturbances; the description of processes is for clinical work much superior to the use of diagnostic psychiatric labels which imply a disease entity, rather than a disturbance of functions and is promising also for the development of clinical theory. Second, it led him to formulate the goal of psychoanalytic therapy: 'Where Id was there Ego shall be.'[23] Like every aphorism, this is an extreme formulation which indicates a direction rather than a realisable goal. By Freud's own description of the id functions—they include some functions which are by definition unavailable to consciousness—they can never be fully replaced by ego functions. Not even everything that once was conscious but has been repressed and is therefore functioning in the peculiarly irrational manner of id functions, can be transformed into ego functions. In the end analysis is interminable. But the direction of effort by analyst and analysand toward a synthesis of total life experience is indicated with the help of this view of personality.

69

In one respect the second, classificatory theory of personality is superior to the first: to look at the mental life of a person from the point of view of unconscious, pre-conscious and conscious mental content can easily be misconstrued as an attempt to isolate the individual as if he existed in a social vacuum. Though Freud himself never fell into this trap even before he arrived at his second formulation—his concentration on the content of mental life as much as his emphasis on the transference situation made him a social psychologist all the way—the recognition of transactions with the real world as a dominant ego function built the social aspects of personality firmly into his conceptual scheme. But the identification of degrees of consciousness was so central to Freud's thought that he felt compelled to combine both approaches. There is, of course, no simple co-ordination between the two descriptions. Indeed, why should there be? The first classification is one of quality of mental process, the second one of purposes. Freud presents the following diagram[24] as a model of 'the structural relations of the mental personality', for which he immediately apologises as an inevitably incorrect representation of the enormous complexities involved.

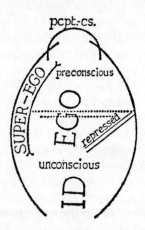

As the diagram indicates, ego functions are partly unconscious (the defence mechanisms), partly pre-conscious and partly conscious; super-ego functions are unconsciously performed but open to becoming pre-conscious and then conscious; id functions are unconsciously executed.

In his previously discussed paper on the Unconscious, Freud distinguished between the descriptive, the dynamic and systematic (theoretical) usage of that term. Even though he did not propose it, the same usages for his personality concept can be evoked. Enough has already been said about the description of personality in these terms. They seem to me an appropriate shorthand for a comprehensive picture of what a human being is all about. It remains to indicate briefly the dynamic and theoretical usage of Freud's personality concept.

Dynamically viewed, Freud's personality concept opens the way to the understanding of conflict—within oneself or with the world around one, or both, in normal as well as in pathological conditions. There can hardly be a 'normal' human being who has never experienced conflict between desire and morality or between his own actions and conscious purposes and those of others. It is of course possible to study man as if the experience of conflict did not exist, at least up to a point; it is even possible to study conflict experiences which normally precede all decision making from a non-dynamic point of view by inferring the existence of conflict from behavioural indicators in rats and men. It is not possible, however, to *understand* inner conflict without some such model as Freud's personality conception in mind, if understanding implies the establishment of a meaningful connection between the phenomenon under study and the total personality which exhibits this phenomenon.

The conflict-free unified self as an enduring state of mind is an idealistic abstraction without much bearing on human experience. Freud's identification of the three groups of functions which constitute the living person serves at least as a heuristic principle in searching for the location of conflicting tendencies. Beyond this it permits comparison of types of conflict however disparate the life situations of individuals may be and is therefore immensely important for clinical practice. Finally it raises major theoretical questions: what must be assumed to determine whether a conflict experience is dominated by id, ego or super-ego functions? Freud's answer to this question lies in his notions of psychic energy and his developmental reconstructions. More of these later.

CHAPTER 5

Psychological Differences Between the Sexes: Inference, Theory or Bias?

FREUD's *Introductory Lectures on Psychoanalysis* retain in print the liveliness and immediacy of the spoken word; they are arguments with his audience rather than cool, systematic exposition. He invariably begins with the phrase 'Meine Damen und Herren'; as he proceeds, in the excitement of proposing an idea, dealing with criticism and refining his original statement, the phrase contracts to 'Meine Herren'.[1] There is no record that the women in his audience had left the room.

To put this delightful slip at the beginning of an examination of Freud's statements on psychological sex differences should only emphasise that the question in the title of this chapter is not rhetorical. Indeed, the enduring and sharp controversy about the validity of Freud's statements on the topic has implications far beyond it. Not only is it at the root of some splits in the psychoanalytic movement (Karen Horney, Clara Thompson and others); not only is it a bone of contention in the women's liberation movement;[2] not only have some of the suggested solutions to the controversy led to a denial of unconscious processes, not to mention the elimination of the idea of the Oedipal complex; beyond its central place in Freud's theory the controversy raises issues for all psychology, perhaps for all sciences: is a culture-free psychology possible? Can man acquire any knowledge uncontaminated by the social and historical conditions of the knower?

The general philosphical debate of these questions provides the overtones to a theme fortunately somewhat simpler: is Freud's view of psychological sex differences the result of the late Victorian era in which he grew up, valid perhaps for

73

that time but only of historical interest today? And did his own personality, over and above a possible cultural bias, induce him to a more persistent distortion than a slip of the tongue?

Like so much of his work, Freud's view of sex differences conveys a search for meaning as well as mechanism; it is profound, provocative, complex, shifting, impossible to ignore in a serious study of the topic, but also ambiguous and inconsistent.

In his lecture on Femininity[3] Freud distinguishes three aspects relevant to the study of sex differences: the biological, the psychological and the cultural. The issue would be relatively simple if biological maleness unequivocally determined psychological maleness which, in turn, determined the social role of males. There is no doubt that this simple assumption has for a long time dominated male and female thought on their respective roles and identities and that even now it has many adherents. Freud explicitly warned against this seductive simplification. But even though biological, psychological and cultural sex identity are not so tightly co-ordinated, most men and women manage to achieve a unifying experience out of these diverse components. It is this experience which is at the centre of Freud's thought.

He begins with the only invariable biological dichotomy in human organisms: the ovum is female, the sperm male; the ovum receives passively, the sperm moves actively. In psychoanalytic terminology, the aim of the sexual instinctual drive in women is passive, in males active. But Freud's notion of instinctual drive is more complex than other usages of the term 'instinct', where it is regarded as an in-built biological tendency. Instinctual drives, in Freud's terminology, are psychological representations of biochemical events, not these events themselves. Instinctual drives so understood are not sufficiently described by their aim; the ways and means of reaching this aim are equally important. In pursuance of the biological aim the identification of male/active and female/passive breaks down. Both sexes can adopt either an active or a passive stance. Other and secondary biological sex differences appear in varying degrees—in contrast to the activity of the sperm, the passivity of the ovum—in both sexes. The recognition of these additional biological factors leads Freud to assert that human beings are, to varying degrees, biologically, psychologically and culturally bi-sexual.[4]

Freud used the notion of psychological bi-sexuality both in an apparently trivial and in an obviously important way. When the development of his thought leads him to make derogatory remarks about psychological femaleness, the presence of women psychoanalysts in his audience induced him to pay them a heavy-handed compliment by suggesting that they possess a high proportion of psychological maleness. But we have learned from Freud that an apparently trivial remark, out of line with the general flow of thoughts, indicates hidden meaning. It is perhaps not too speculative to suggest that Freud felt uneasy about some of his conclusions, that he sensed a flaw somewhere in the argument which he could not resolve, for he himself admitted on several occasions that he was baffled by the psychology of women. He explicitly excludes the task of defining psychological femininity as inappropriate. Here and elsewhere he emphasises that definitions may be the outcome, but they are certainly not the starting point of an enquiry in which one gropes, motivated by the wish to understand, with changing assumptions towards greater clarity.

But the clear importance of the assumption of bi-sexuality lies in the fact that it forms the bedrock of the fundamental psychoanalytic question with regard to sex differences: how does a newborn baby, who must certainly not be credited with having a psychological representation of his sexual equipment, but who has a bi-sexual psychological potential, develop a psychological identity as a man or a woman? The question so formulated indicates immediately that Freud conceived of the process not as a foregone conclusion, not as the inevitable unfolding of maturation, but as an active interplay between the child and varying sequences of external events; hence a process beset by difficulties whose mastery or

75

mere endurance determines the type of sexual identification which is ultimately achieved.

Freud asserts that in the first three or so years of life there is little, if any, difference between boys and girls in the expression of their infantile sexuality. The term 'infantile sexuality, so central to Freud's developmental theory, requires explanation.[5] The very fact that Freud distinguishes infantile sexuality from genital sexuality clearly indicates that he was not attributing to a small boy the wish to have sexual intercourse with his mother; if that had been his opinion the adjectives 'infantile' and 'genital' applied to sexuality would have been redundant and misleading. In Freud's thoughts sexuality was a superordinate notion of which infantile and genital modes were distinct subcategories. Whilst he always held fast to the logic of this terminology, he left the superordinate meaning of sexuality largely implicit, thereby encouraging misunderstandings of the crudest kind. However, George Klein, a psychoanalyst and experimental psychologist, has distilled from Freud's writings his essential conception of sexuality: '. . . the shared factor of infantile and adult sexuality . . . is a capacity for a *primary, distinctively poignant, pleasure experience* capable of manifesting itself from infancy on . . . it is evocable from direct stimulation of the dermal surface of the body . . . (it) is a positive aspect of a distinctive excitatory process of a body zone, and it is different from the pleasurable experiences of satisfaction or of reward.'[6] Klein can identify some statements in Freud's *Three Essays on the Theory of Sexuality*[7] where Freud specifically refers to the kinesthetic pleasure *sui generis* which constitutes sexuality, and he rightly points out that the whole organisation of this work rests on this conception. If infantile sexuality were identical with genital sexuality, the whole idea of a developmental approach to it would be nonsense. Infantile sexuality has nothing but the sensual pleasure derived from the stimulation of body zones in common with the vast variety of experiences and ideas that are involved in adult genital sexuality; but adult sexuality in its diversity of manifestations can retain features of its infantile precursor. Some of these are culturally positively sanctioned, others negatively sanctioned (oral versus anal pleasures).

From this notion of infantile sexuality follow the well known developmental stages, oral, anal, phallic and genital sexuality. Babies of both sexes receive their first sexual pleasure from the stimulation of the oral zone through nipple or bottle. It would credit the infant with the logical competence of the adult to imagine that he can, at that early stage, localise the source of pleasure to the stimulation of the mucous membrane of lips and mouth. It is the whole situation, including the mother, which provides the first infantile sexual pleasure. Accordingly both sexes form a profound attachment to the mother from this experience. Many well meaning critics have suggested that this same process called love for the mother, rather than infantile sexuality, would have created less hostility and misunderstanding. But as indicated above there is more involved than 'the shock treatment of honesty',[8] as Philip Rieff calls Freud's insistence on his own terminology, a statement which implies that Freud was more concerned with making an impact on a 'shock-treated' audience than with the ideas themselves.

The next body zone on which adult influence concentrates the child's attention is the anus. The inevitability is social rather than biological; it is the mother rather than the child who derives benefit from successful toilet training. Here the psychological situation, still common to both sexes, is already much more complex. Even if at the age of two years or more the child can be assumed to be able to localise the body-source of the sensual pleasure inherent in retaining or passing faeces, the adult world is intimately associated with the regulation of this experience. Parents, mostly mothers, start making demands on the emerging conceptual organisation of the young child, to appeal to the nascent ego functions to keep to social rules. A good performance is rewarded, a bad one punished. The child, still free from the socially acquired emotion of disgust, is interested in the product of his body which is linked to the experience of pleasure and obviously

77

regarded as important by his guardians; he plays with his excrements. Once again adult vetoes are as inevitable as they are hard for the child to understand, an early example of the experience of conflict. The range of emotional experiences linked to the child's discovery of the anus as a source of sexual pleasure is already wide: a sense of achievement or of failure, the experience of rewards and frustrations which go with both, defiance and obedience,[9] of being loved or unloved are closely associated with it, experiences which now also begin to be associated with the oral zone. For the various stages in the development of sexuality do not necessarily replace each other but can continue into adult life as sources of pleasure.

Simultaneously or later the child of course discovers the special sensitivity of the genitalia as a source for pleasurable stimulation, hence the virtual ubiquity of early masturbation. At the age of three or four this is the major form of autoerotic gratification. Freud terms it the phallic stage in contrast to the still distant final genital stage. Whether 'phallic' is the right term for the experience of both sexes is a moot point not to be pursued here, for in any case this is the moment when Freud begins to differentiate the sexual development of both sexes, speaking with confident certainty about the boy's, and hesitatingly and with many afterthoughts about that of the girl.

The boy enters the period of the Oedipus complex. The dramatic name Freud gave to this sequence of developmental events has become so powerful a focus of Freudian thought that to question its appropriateness with intent to replace it would be futile. The grand analogy contained in this nomenclature, so typical of Freud's mind, has however not only the virtues but also the liabilities of all analogy. Sophocles' King Oedipus is, of course, the tragedy of an adult. It encourages the confusion between infantile and adult sexuality. Some of the most interesting comments on the Oedipus complex remain on that level. Schorske,[9] for example, who concludes from an analysis of Freud's political dreams in truly Freudian fashion that he must have been beset by a deep ambivalence *vis-à-vis* political authority, draws attention to the fact that Freud used only the sexual aspects of the Oedipal legend with the effect of 'neutralising politics . . . Sophocles' *Oedipus Rex* is unthinkable except as a *res publica*, with its real hero motivated by political obligation: to remove the plague from Thebes.' However interesting the political meaning of *Oedipus Rex* and Schorske's deductions about Freud's political oedipal complex, these are aspects of his adult mind, not within the range of possible experiences during stages of infantile sexuality. Equally, on the adult level Ricoeur[10] draws attention to the fact that King Oedipus has such profound appeal even to modern audiences not only, as Freud suggested, because we unconsciously realise that his tragedy was what we longed for in childhood, but because it reveals that all adult self-knowledge is inherently tragic; before Oedipus knew he did not suffer.

Even though the comments of both these authors are, in their context, more profound than here indicated, it would be well to put them deliberately aside in the present context, together with Sophocles' Jocasta who says that many sons dream of sleeping with their mothers. This they may well do as adults, and the dream may be a consequence of the particular manner in which they dealt with their early oedipal experience. But sleeping with one's mother in the adult technical sense of having sexual intercourse with her is beyond the cognitive competence of the mind of a three or four year old boy.

There are two factors in that age period on which most developmental psychologists as well as sensitive lay observers of small children are in agreement. First, the three to five year old child has an enormous and occasionally frightening repertoire of intense and passionate emotions. Fits of despair, temper tantrums, jealousy, unbridled love and hate bear witness to the intensity of emotion which the small child can experience. Second, though nowhere so called in Freud's writings, the cognitive ability of the small child is very restricted, notwithstanding the great achievement of language acquisition. In Piaget's terms he is in the pre-operational

79

stage, tied to his perceptions, already searching for explanations but not yet able to stand back from the immediacy of his own sense impressions, and much preoccupied with achieving mastery over his own body and growing strength. Freud comes nearest to drawing explicitly upon the immature level of the child's cognitive development as an essential feature of the oedipal phase in his essay 'On the Sexual Theories of Children'.[11]

Probably already before that period a little boy has discovered his penis as a most remarkable body organ from which all sorts of pleasure can be derived. That this organ which behaves so visibly differently from arms or legs should not arouse the boy's special interest is almost inconceivable.

In Freud's famous case history of Little Hans[12] interest in the penis leads to an intellectual discovery, the difference between major categories in the external world: horses and people have 'widdlers', Little Hans remarks, 'but tables and chairs do not'. As with every intellectual discovery, first generalisations need to be qualified and so he asks his mother if she, too, has a 'widdler'. The silly woman says yes. But a little boy would have to be very stupid not to discover the morphological sex difference. There is the position in urinating, there may be a little sister, observation of animals, or views of the parent's body. Sooner or later the small child acquires perfectly correct knowledge: boys and men have a visible penis, girls and women do not. For the small boy the penis as a source of pleasure becomes a highly valued possession. Since the earliest experience of sexual pleasure occurs in a cognitive context of which the mother is an essential feature, since the boy is already profoundly attached to her, he wants to associate her with the newly discovered phallic pleasure; he wants to be touched by her, sleep in her bed, replace the father there, wish him dead or away so that he could 'marry' his mother. But he does not want to insert his penis in her because he cannot possibly have an adequate image of this rather complex physical act. As Freud said: 'childish love has no bounds but also no aim. It is doomed to disappointment.'[13] These then are the basic psychological ingredients of the oedipal conflict: passionate but aimless sensual attachment to the mother; jealousy of the father or a sibling in intimate bodily contact with the mother, combined with phantasies about the death or disappearance of the rival.

But the child's growing power of observation and his cognitive development do not stop. Soon he begins to wonder why his beloved mother is without a penis. It is hardly surprising that his theory building is taken from his direct experience, whatever correct or foolish answer adults may provide to direct questions. In any case, it is not easy to give an adequate answer to the *why* of sex differentiation. What is within a small boy's cognitive scope is the experience that treasured objects can be given, but also taken away as a punishment by all-powerful adults. Even when no direct castration threat is made, the idea of things being taken away is, at this stage, a perfectly reasonable explanation for absence. If the penis was taken away from females, the boy's own may be in equal danger. This terrifying fear of loss of the penis is, of course, in Freud's terminology the castration complex. Putting two and two together on the concrete perceptual level of the developing mind leads to logical conclusions from the only available premises: if the mother has suffered the terrible fate of losing her penis, she is not as strong or powerful as the father. The little boy begins to turn to him as the better protector, to want to be like him who has kept his penis. The castration complex has led to the resolution of that part of the oedipal complex which produces hostility to the father; it is replaced by an identification with his own sex; it is this identification which encourages the internalisation of parental standards and thus establishes the foundation of the super-ego.

What about the development of the small girl? With considerable hesitation and profound uncertainty this is how, in the end, Freud describes female development in these crucial years. The girl's early attachment to the mother is equal in intensity to that of the boy. Her specific new source of sensual pleasure in the phallic stage is masturbation of the clitoris.

But she can hardly escape the discovery that what boys have to play with is bigger and within her concrete, perception-bound cognitive limits, better for all she knows. Her explanations for the difference are similar to those of the boy, but while he feels privileged though threatened, she feels under-privileged. In her case, the castration complex, that is the idea that an object her brother possesses has been taken away from her, occurs while she is still passionately attached to her mother, i.e. a person of her own sex. The result of her discovery is envy, Freud's famous concept of penis envy.

Now a psychological difficulty sets in which boys do not have to face; a boy can continue his attachment to his mother while wishing to be like his father so as to love her like he does. The girl, on the other hand, must somehow learn to abandon her first great love in favour of her father, must identify with the mother even though being female appears to her mind at that stage as an under-privileged position because of the absence of the penis. She must learn to convert her penis envy into love for those who have it. In contrast to the boy where oedipal attachment to the mother precedes the castration complex, her passionate oedipal attachment follows the 'discovery' of her castration and the accompanying feelings of envy and of resentment against her fate as a female. In the end, if things go well, envy changes into the wish to have a baby.

Once again it should be emphasised that these shifting, powerful and complex experiences occur on the conceptual level of the three, four or five year old who lacks the vocabulary for putting into words what pains or delights him, a fact which undoubtedly contributes to the amnesia of most people for the passions of early childhood; that he is nonetheless groping to understand and forms theories appropriate to his developmental stage; and that bodily pleasures occur within a social context which stimulates curiosity, comparisons and the attribution of meaning to the relations in his immediate social environment.

In view of the fact that unaided adult memory is, as a rule, unable to confirm these fascinating hypothesised events which have obvious bearing on psychological sex differences, the question arises: is one to believe all this, at least as a plausible construction? After all Freud himself inferred these notions not from direct observation of children, but retrospectively from his adult patients, most of whom he found he could understand best through discovering that they were struggling with unresolved problems stemming from the phallic stage.

There are three justifications for believing that this is a reasonable approximation of the sexual, cognitive and emotional development of both sexes. The first lies in the previously noted consensus on the general psychological characteristics of this developmental stage: while there exists a great capacity for the experience and expression of passionate emotions, cognitive abilities develop only slowly and gradually, and there is much evidence from developmental research for the unconventionality, compared to adult thought, of early conceptualisations.

Second, from a broad perspective, there is a similarity between Freud and Piaget in their approach to the child's construction of reality. It is true, Freud did not occupy himself with cognitive development outside the sphere of family and particularly sexuality; Piaget does not deal either with emotions or with the possibility of individual differences. But they were both equally concerned with the interaction from outside and inside the boundary of the skin, with the child's attribution of meaning to the world around him, and above all with a child-centred point of view, in tacit recognition that the nature of the construction put on reality is always a function of the abilities of the construer; however inadequate the child's construction may appear to an adult, for the child it fills the function of reality since it serves as a basis for his actions and experiences. It should not be beyond the power of psychologists to adapt Piaget's imaginative exploratory techniques to the child's construction of a world composed of two sexes in order to demonstrate the extent to which the Freudian reconstructions are correct descriptions of the child's view of sex differences. It is possible, by the way, that Freud somewhat underrated in the oedipal and castration complexes of both sexes the influence on the child of cross-sex parental preferences, which he mentions only in passing and which is the rule in many families. The erotic component in fatherly love for a daughter and motherly love for a son, so often described in literature, may well be a significant influence on the manner in which the child masters these early challenges and this should not be too difficult to demonstrate.

Third, and notwithstanding the fact that systematic verification is as yet sparse, the validity of Freud's constructions is open to systematic investigation by studying the hypothesised consequences of these early events in later life. For it goes without saying that Freud's entire intellectual enterprise is intended to be explanatory, not just descriptive. It stands or falls on the power to understand later development in the light of earlier events. Contrary to popularisations of psychoanalysis Freud explicitly acknowledges that sexual and personality development does not stop with the passing of castration and oedipal complexes.[14] But the early representations of events and ideas are, as a rule, repressed and continue to exercise influence where id functions dominate. The question arises, then, whether there is any systematic evidence for consequences in later experiences and behaviour which could be expected if oedipal feelings, castration fear or penis envy were actually experienced in early childhood.

Kline[15] has examined most of the empirical evidence for the existence of consequences to be expected if Freud's theory of sexual development of both sexes were correct. He arrives at the conclusion that there is some good evidence for both the oedipal and castration complexes. He quotes, for example, a study by Hall and colleagues who derived from Freud's account the hypothesis that adult men should have more dreams symbolically expressing castration anxiety and women more of wanting to castrate, thus expressing penis envy. They found their hypothesis strongly confirmed by the dreams of 120 male and female college students.

But what does Freud himself deduce from his reconstructions of early sexual development for the adult character of men and women?

Here, it seems to me, he is on less acceptable ground. In his description of early development Freud is very careful to point out how at that stage things can go wrong for boys and girls—strong fixations on one of the stages at the expense of another, choice of other sex parent for identification, same sex parent as love object which may lead to homosexuality, self as love object with resulting narcissism and inability to love another, unresolved castration anxiety or penis envy, etc.—as well as how they can go right. In his generalisations about psychological femininity, however, he seems to have forgotten the possibility of a constructive solution to these early complexes, at least for women. Psychological bisexuality drops out of the picture; in his concluding remarks in his lecture on femininity he somewhat grudgingly admits that apart from determination by her sexual function, '. . . an individual woman may be [note: not is] a human being in other respects as well . . .'[16] Apparently he did not think it very probable that a woman at ease with her own sexual identity could also acquire a distinct identity as a person beyond the sexual sphere.

With some cautionary remarks against overgeneralisations he nevertheless proceeds to state that because of the virtually inevitable experience of early penis envy, women develop a number of not altogether desirable psychological characterisations: they are more vain, compensating for their early discovered inferiority by overvaluing their beauty and externalities; they experience more shame, which has the function of hiding the absence of a penis; they want to be loved rather than love; they are less creative and have little sense of justice since their basic envy interferes; they are weaker in their social interests and have less capacity for sublimation, are more rigid, age earlier psychologically, are less sincere as well as intellectually inferior.

The point to be made about this collective portrait of woman has nothing to do with whether or not it was a largely correct description of the majority of women in Freud's time. It may well have been so; for all one knows it may even be true today, as Juliet Mitchell[17] seems to think. Freud did certainly not base his view on anything approaching statistical data which in this area are as unavailable now as they were then. Rather he presents his notion of women as following directly as deductions from his description of the development of infantile sexuality. It is the correctness and the completeness of this psychological reasoning process which is at question.

Accepting Freud's construction of childhood events as reasonable, and remaining on a Freudian basis, are there not other, equally plausible deductions possible? Would not men, overcompensating for their early castration fears, develop excessive vanity with regard to their maleness? If the little girl learns early in life that one can exist, has to exist, without owning everything in sight, would she not overcompensate this originally painful discovery by becoming generous, making a virtue out of necessity? If the little girl's oedipal complex occurs later than that of the boy, as Freud plausibly suggests, that is at a stage of greater cognitive and verbal ability, would she not be more open to remaining in touch with her unconscious and be capable of more empathy? Again on the assumption of a later oedipal experience would she not, more than a boy, retain the marvellous childhood advantage of managing to combine sexuality and tenderness and therefore be less likely to develop sadistic brutality?

These questions are not rhetorical: I do not claim that the implied suggestions present a more adequate picture of women's psychological attributes than Freud's, only that with similar psychological premises a less negatively tinged view could emerge. He may well have been right, but for the wrong reason.

Inevitably one must ask what went wrong in Freud's essay on femininity, and why. Nothing in Freud's life experience, as far as he saw fit to communicate it, points to a personal bias against women. On the contrary: this first and adored son of a beautiful young woman married a woman with whom he was passionately in love, was apparently satisfied in his marriage,[18] became a loving father of three sons and three daughters one of whom was intellectually brilliant, and was capable of deep friendships with other women.[19] His case histories of women patients abound in descriptions of their intelligence, vivacity, wide-ranging interests and devotion to social activities. The image he presented can certainly not be regarded as a generalisation of his clinical practice. It is true, his first women patients landed him in a traumatic intellectual and public confusion by presenting their phantasies of early seductions as actual memories of events. But since he was able to derive from his final understanding of these false memories decisive intellectual progress, not even this episode is an excuse for assuming that personal experience is an adequate explanation of his one-sided view of the female character.

What happened, one must assume, is that Freud unwittingly succumbed to the prevailing cultural stereotype of women, mistaking their historical role for the essence of femininity. He thought he understood the beginning of their development; he saw in the social stereotype what he regarded as the inevitable outcome; he therefore felt justified in seeking for psychological processes only to the extent that they confirmed the inevitable. Nothing but powerful culturally imposed assumptions, all the more powerful because, in the context of this discussion of the female character, Freud did not question them, can explain an error of logic in one of Freud's most profound late essays, 'Analysis Terminable and Interminable'.[20] There he says that analysis as a therapy 'is most difficult when trying to persuade a woman to abandon her wish for a penis or convince a man that passive attitudes towards another man are sometimes indispensable'. Note the asymmetry in formulation: men need to be persuaded of the legitimacy of psychological bi-sexuality, while women have to abandon the idea of psychological bi-sexuality. 'The wish for a penis', like so much else in Freud's terminology, is a *pars pro toto* term, meaning psychological activeness. And even though Freud had warned in his lecture on femininity against assuming that biological passivity was leading to psychological passivity, even though he had there pointed out that the passive biological aim (i.e. the passivity of the ovum) can be very actively pursued, the phrase quoted shows that he did not really convince himself of the lack of parallel between the biological and the psychological spheres.

To detect a profound cultural bias in this respect is relatively easy with the advantage of hindsight several decades later during which a dramatic revolution of values attached to femininity and masculinity has occurred. One need not identify with the lunatic fringe of the women's liberation movement in order to assert confidently that a very large number of modern women are acquiring psychological bisexuality; but one has to distance oneself decidedly from them in their treatment of Freud. What they do not understand is that notwithstanding the radical change in adult sexual values, the childhood processes remain unaffected by this. Women's liberation does not change the early emotion- and image-laden discoveries of one's own body and the meanings attributed to morphological sex differences which Freud postulated as rooted in the attributes of the developing human organism, including its slow cognitive development. Perhaps this fact may be changed in evolutionary time-spans,[21] but not in parallel with historical changes. Given this more enduring process, a model of how adaptation to a changed cultural situation evolves from the early experiences of castration fear and penis envy remains to be constructed. It is an open question whether the achievement of psychological femininity different from Freud's character portrait will be more or less demanding in terms of ego strength and, therefore, whether it will lead to more or less neuroses in women; it may well change in decades to come a feature of society which was as basic in Freud's time as it is now: the nuclear family, and thereby the possibility of passionate attachment of the infant to the mother which is so crucial to Freud's view of achieving sexual identity or failing to do so. Even so radical a change, however, would not alter the fact that every child has to discover anew the existence and meaning of morphological sex differences.

When Freud, with all his contradictions, deliberately

turned his great mind to an examination of the cultural situation as he knew it, he emerged once again as a radical and revolutionary thinker, no longer tied to the status quo, no longer essentially conservative as he was in accepting the stereotype about women (as well as in his political views.)[22]

In 1908 Freud wrote an essay entitled 'Civilised Sexual Morality and Modern Nervous Illness'.[23] It is a remarkable essay in more than one way. He quotes there, in some detail, a book by Christian Ehrenfels, the first Gestalt psychologist who, like Binet (but in contrast to many later psychologists), recognised the power of sexuality in man's fate, its legitimate place in psychology, and drew attention to the noxious influences of what was then regarded as civilised sexual morality. The essay deals with the hypocritical double standard for men's and women's sexual behaviour which, Freud said, enforced deception of self and others and led to neuroses, particularly in women for whom it is more difficult to break the moral code because of the possibility of pregnancy before marriage or where sexual relations in marriage had ceased; abstinence, Freud claims, is harder to bear for women because they have less possibility for sublimation. Indeed, Freud sounds here almost like a champion of women's causes when he says that the 'undoubted intellectual inferiority of so many women can . . . be traced back to the inhibition of thought necessitated by sexual repression.'[24] No biological inferiority is implied here. There then follows a quite ferocious denunciation of the institution of monogamy because of the virtually intolerable burden it imposes on adult sexuality, leaving women sexually deeply frustrated and leading young men either to the same fate or to an exploitation of working-class girls in secret liaisons, to prostitutes, and this at the time of widespread prevalence and justified dread of venereal disease for which no cure existed.[25]

One can well imagine that this essay contributed to Freud's undeserved reputation of advocating 'free love', and that some people must have been infuriated by Freud's condemnation of the hypocrisy by which they lived and from which they suffered, since he could not show them an easy way out. Sublimation, after all, is not achievable on command. One may understand such fury, but it is decidedly not the proper condition for reading Freud. Philip Rieff was right when he made morality the major characteristic of Freud's mind. The outburst against monogamy was not equivalent to an advocacy of immorality. Freud discusses here for the first time a theme which he was to take up much later in *Civilization and Its Discontents*,[26] the relation between civilisation and the suppression of instinctual drives. On the assumption that sexuality does not just serve the purposes of reproduction, but aims at gaining a particular type of pleasure, he searches for a type of sexual morality which does not require as much suppression as the moral code of his time which, in any case, was self-defeating since the standards could not be met, unless one accepted the prevalence of neurosis as not too high a price to pay for civilisation.

It is true that Freud abdicates as it were at this stage by pointing out that the development of such a new moral code is not the task of psychology, perhaps overlooking his own earlier contribution to stipulating the realistic conditions under which such a code could come into being. For already before the turn of the century he had expressed an almost optimistic view on how things might change for the better. In 1898 he wrote: '. . . it would be one of the greatest triumphs of mankind, one of the most tangible liberations from the bondage of nature to which we are subject, were it possible to raise the responsible act of procreation to the level of a voluntary and intentional act, and to free it from its entanglement with an indispensable satisfaction of a natural desire.'[27] We are, of course, with the help of new technologies of contraception approaching a period where this is possible for many millions. If Freud was right in his social diagnosis, some sources of adult sexual frustration and some of the hypocrisy of society are on the way out.

At the beginning of this chapter the question was raised as to whether Freud's view on psychological sex differences was of more than historical interest. The answer is neither a simple yes or no. His view of adult femininity is very much in keeping with both the popular and the scientific stereotypes of his time; the latter has been persuasively documented by Stephanie Shields for the period from the middle of the nineteenth century to the first third of the twentieth century.[28] So much agreement on this negative stereotype may, for all one knows, reflect the actual characteristics of women at the time. This is not the issue, however. Where the brain physiologists, statisticians, philosophers and Freud went wrong was in the attribution of a biological causality which ignored cultural and historical constraints in their impact on adult behaviour and character.[29]

His model of psychological sex differentiation in childhood, however, is on a different plane, precisely because its major premise is a-historical, namely the coexistence in the early years of a human being of a vast repertoire of emotion with a limited scope of cognitive ability. No other model of child development has managed to combine these two undisputed aspects of early childhood. In addition, the categories of thought which Freud brings to bear on this situation are important, whatever the historical situation. What are these categories?

First there is the recognition of the fundamental unity of body and mind: the discovery of one's own body which inevitably has different results for each sex and leads to concept and theory formation in the child. Even if the languages in which body and mind are described must differ and psychology cannot be reduced to physiology without loss of vital information,[30] all experience is possible only within a body. Second there is Freud's insistence on sexuality as the great power in emotional life, in sharp contrast to the aseptic view on sex differences, which pervades so much academic research on the topic. Passion, tamed and untamed, is the subject of his thought, not stimulus and response. Third, and here he is in line with academic child psychology, Freud insists that an important way to the understanding of human beings is to trace the processes through which they became what they are. These categories of thought jointly describe

Freud's approach to the study of sex differences. An approach is, of course, in principle untestable; one can only take it or leave it. Freud's more concrete descriptions of the developmental sequence are often so intermingled with basic assumptions beyond those singled out above that it requires considerable ingenuity to distinguish the testable and the untestable. But it has been done as indicated before with mixed results, some providing confirmation and some not. Much more could and should be done in this area.

At present one can only speculate whether the concrete answers which Freud provides on infantile sexuality will be changed or modified by new historical circumstances. Nowadays there are a number of families in which the father undertakes the nurturing role while the mother goes out to work. If the child's first passionate attachment is to the nurturing person, whatever will help the little boy develop the ability to love a woman? Will the sexual development of a girl be made easier since she need not abandon her first love object? Is it conceivable that the full availability of both parents for both sexes in infancy as figures of first attachment might mitigate the troubles and sufferings which now so often accompany the acquisition of sexual identity? Only time will tell; Freud did not consider such possibilities.

CHAPTER 6

Metapsychology: Explanation or Explicandum?

FREUD used his idiosyncratic term 'metapsychology' in various ways. It appears first before the turn of the century in his letters to Fliess; in one of them he asks his friend 'whether I should use the term "metapsychology" for my psychology which leads behind consciousness'.[1] The context in which this question is put makes the meaning of the term puzzling. Freud talks about his work on *The Interpretation of Dreams* and says: 'It seems to me as if the wish-fulfilment theory gives only the psychological and not the biological, or rather metapsychological explanation.' Fliess, apparently, did not persuade Freud to abandon the term, for it remained within the psychoanalytic vocabulary and came into its own years later in Freud's papers on metapsychology.[2] There, according to Jones,[3] it implies 'a comprehensive description of any mental process', while David Rapaport[4] reads it to mean 'the study of the assumptions upon which the system of psychoanalytic theory is based'; in another publication, however, he identified metapsychology as the 'principles in psychoanalytic theory'.[5] Hartmann, who apparently felt uneasy about the term, defines it as theory on the highest level of abstraction.[6] Strachey,[7] in the editorial introduction to the papers on metapsychology, uses the slightly odd phrase 'views on psychological theory' to characterise metapsychology, obviously implying something different from the theory itself. Hilgard seems to suggest that metapsychology is a collection of Freud's models of man,[8] and Laplanche and Pontalis[9] say that 'metapsychology constructs an ensemble of conceptual models which are more or less far-removed from empirical reality'.

The effort of clarifying the meaning and relation to each other of scientific terms such as description, assumption, principle, explanation, theory and model would involve entering a field in which only epistomologists do not fear to tread, and even they emerge with differing answers. In such a dilemma one turns again to Freud's own writings in search of clarification. After all, he was not an epistomologist either. There one meets another term which at first sight complicates understanding, but on second thought may lead to a consistent and simpler reading of what metapsychology means; in spite of its simplicity it does not diminish but rather accentuates the profundity of Freud's thought. This term is 'point of view'. The phrase which Freud and, following him, the great theoreticians of psychoanalysis use repeatedly is 'metapsychological points of view'. Such juxtaposition of the abstruse with the colloquial sounds almost funny, particularly since neither term had at the time entered the vocabulary of other psychologists. But such other psychologists have their points of view too, even if they do not make them explicit as a rule, and certainly do not call them metapsychological. Nonetheless, what distinguishes outstanding psychologists from one another on the most general level is precisely this: the point from which they view man. In other words, they differ from each other most in terms of the fundamental question about man which they have chosen as focus for their work. The nature of this basic question guides their investigations and determines the broad categories of answers they find, if not the answer itself. For example, Skinner's basic question is to ask how the environment shapes behaviour; Piaget's how the child acquires complex thought processes; physiological psychologists' what the organismic processes are which underlie behaviour and experience; Adler's how the will to power determines a person's life; and Jung perhaps raises the eternal and unanswerable question: what is man? These are their points of view or, if preferred, their metapsychological stances; 'meta' this time in analogy to metaphysics, for the basic viewpoint from which man is studied is adopted for reasons which go beyond their own psychological theories.

Whatever theories are developed under such differing

points of view will, of course, explain only the phenomena subsumed in a psychologist's fundamental question. This is why it is quite pointless to try an evaluative comparison between, say, Skinner and physiological psychologists. They ask questions from incompatible points of view, however legitimate each question in itself may be.

The extraordinary aspect of Freud's work is that he was not limited to one point of view, that he asked several fundamental questions, and asked them in the spirit of a scientist, that is 'not interested in the ultimate "nature" or "essence" of such processes—whatever this may mean—[but] in finding a conceptual framework for the phenomena he had discovered'.[10]

In what follows an effort will be made to account for Freud's several metapsychological points of view by identifying the major concern or questions to which each of them corresponds, that is the psychological phenomena which struck him as requiring explanation. In other words, the metapsychology is here regarded as Freud's implied conception of the subject matter of psychology.

Even though Kris[11] sees the metapsychology already contained in the *Project for a Scientific Psychology* written in 1895, Freud did not start his psychological thought with it in mind. The direction of his theoretical curiosities evolved gradually from his phenomenological involvement with his early patients. Originally geared only to the task of helping them, he immersed himself in all aspects of the lives of these complex and troubled people. He saw before him the answers; but what were the questions? Groping for formulations was an immensely difficult task, for there existed no adequate vocabulary to convey the psychological meaning he sensed in his patients' odd behaviour. Gradually he created the language of psychoanalysis, a mixture of common-sense terms with special meaning, the scientific vocabulary of his time, and neologisms of which 'metapsychological points of view' is an example.[12] He himself identified only three of the latter —the dynamic, the economic and the topographical. Implicit in his work are three more which Rapaport named the genetic, the structural and the adaptive points of view. What are the fundamental psychological questions and concerns underlying each of them?

The phenomenon to which the dynamic point of view is relevant is the experience of conflict, ubiquitous not only in patients but in everybody's effort to cope with life. Notwithstanding the universality of the experience, academic psychology has not made this a central topic of research. Indeed, Freud's insistence on the complexity of man with his manifold and conflicting motivations is probably the most distinguishing attribute of psychoanalytic thought. Granted that every scientific enterprise is an effort to simplify the complexity of the phenomenal world, there is a limit beyond which this effort must not be carried: there must remain a link, however long stretched and tenuous, between the simplified formulation and the subject matter to which it refers. If conflict is as central to human functioning as Freud assumed, psychological theories which simplify it out of existence remain, at best, incomplete. Freud's dynamic simplifications did not outstep these limits. He conceptualised his answer to the basic question: why conflict? in terms of mental forces: 'Our purpose is not merely to describe and classify the phenomena, but to conceive them as brought about by the play of forces in the mind . . . which work together or against one another. We are endeavouring to attain a *dynamic conception* of mental phenomena.'[13]

This, it should be noted, is the point where not only much academic psychology but also the existentialists part company with Freud, from whose phenomenology they had learned so much. Neither for Sartre nor for Laing is the idea of identifiable conflicting forces a central problem. In their holistic view of man he is what he is and his own consciousness is the sum total of permissible evidence. In Freud's analytic view these forces can be identified by interpreting the meaning of behaviour and experience as a compromise between tendencies pulling man in different directions, even if his awareness is restricted to the experience of conflict without knowing what gave rise to it. Inference to unconscious processes is required to understand the complexity of psychological conflict even when it is as trivial as being in a dilemma about whether to work or play, let alone in pathological conflict such as, for example, knowing that one's hands are clean but feeling compelled to wash them again and again. Rapaport,[14] in an effort to systematise the psychoanalytic theory of motivation, mentions the following relatively concrete psychological issues for which the dynamic point of view is required: how does one account for the content of pathological phenomena? How for irrational non-pathological thought and behaviour? How for the peremptory character of some thoughts and behaviour, that is for their compelling quality which does not leave room for choice (e.g. disgust at the sight of, say, worms; or perfectionism)? How for the emergence of 'spontaneous' images, ideas or action tendencies (i.e. not produced by external reality)? Now it is, of course, possible to engage in constructive psychological thought while ignoring such questions. If they are admitted as relevant psychological topics, however, it is not easy to see how they could be tackled without a dynamic approach based on the identification of potentially conflicting psychological forces.

The legitimacy of the question about irrationality needs comment since psychoanalytic arguments have been used to suggest that this concept be ruled out of court. Hartmann[15] criticises such attempts and summarises the faulty argument as follows: 'since psychoanalysis has shown that the behaviour of neurotics, and even of psychotics, is meaningful . . . what previously was thought to be irrational action is proved to be not irrational at all, and the term, therefore, is misleading . . .' It is true that psychoanalytic propositions are designed to reveal the method in the madness, that is the unconscious reason for what is consciously experienced and observed as without reason or justified by insufficient reasons. That the irrational can be transformed into the rational, that is that sufficient reasons can be discovered, is certainly no justification, however, for denying its original existence. Irrationality remains an important concept, restricted to the functioning of the secondary process in consciousness, when it can be demonstrated that the reasons given are not good enough to explain an action; it serves as an indicator of interference by processes outside consciousness. It need hardly be said that the elimination of irrationality is neither possible nor desirable. However important it is from a reflective point of view to distinguish rational from irrational actions, living on the rational level only impoverishes existence. Rational and irrational are concepts applicable uniquely only to man. Animals pursuing their desires without semantic transformation are neither rational nor irrational.

To begin with Freud's elaboration of the dynamic point of view concentrated on man's instinctual drives and their vicissitudes. The theory underwent many changes, and it is not always clear whether new formulations were meant as substitutes or additions to earlier conceptions. His late postulations of life and death instincts in *Beyond the Pleasure Principle*[16] conceive of instinct in a biological sense. However, for the dynamic question of motivations his earlier concept 'instinctual drive' as a psychological phenomenon remains central.[17] By it he means the *psychological representations* which somatic sources achieve in the mind. In contrast to, say, the biological instinct for breathing which is satisfied by air alone, the instinctual drives have an enormous range of objects which can meet their aim. The description of the development of sexuality in children in the previous chapter has already shown how early gratification is linked inextricably to the objects in the world in which the child lives. Instinctual drives are therefore clearly social-psychological phenomena. The understanding of motivation involves unravelling the meaning which vast numbers of real objects in the real world acquire in an ever-enlarging chain of additions and substitutions; they gratify instinctual drives as they also enlarge the child's knowledge of the real world. In this sense the pleasure and reality principles as rules for human conduct are not necessarily antagonistic to each other, for in the pleasure of reaching an instinctual aim the child discovers the reality of the world. But there often is antagonism between pleasure and reality, for the reality in which the child achieved, or at least sought pleasure changes as he reaches adulthood; the search for gratification appropriate to his early experience is no longer so under new conditions. Yet the early pattern may persist, hidden from consciousness. In the 'timeless' unconscious not only early compromises endure but also unresolved conflicts, say, between sexuality and aggression, between love and hate.

Freud's dynamic approach to motivation led him to develop several theories of a somewhat lower range: on aggression, on defence mechanisms, on narcissism, and others. Its distinctive characteristic is the assumption that conflict is inherent in the instinctual equipment of the human organism. Freud in his concentration on the vicissitudes of instinctual drives, however, could be accused of eliminating fate from the affairs of man. It is not only from the inside-out but also from the outside-in that the dynamics of human conflict and motivation must be understood. Only relatively late in his life did Freud explicitly concern himself with external causes of behaviour. Rapaport[18] in discussing these issues draws attention to a footnote Freud added in 1925 to *The Interpretation of Dreams*: '. . . It cannot be disputed that in the course of an analysis various events may occur the responsibility for which cannot be laid upon the patient's intentions. His father may die without his having murdered him . . . Even if the interrupting event is a real one and independent of the patient, it often depends on him how great an interruption it causes . . .' The systematic elaboration of the interplay between internally and externally originating dynamic forces remained to be done by Freud's successors, Rapaport, Hartmann and particularly Erikson, even though Freud's case studies implicitly recognise the importance of external events.

The dynamic point of view is in sharp contrast to many studies of motivation by academic psychologists even when they are concerned with an appropriate balance between inside and outside. Bindra and Stewart,[19] for example, describe recent advances in the study of motivation as follows: 'The view of motivational processes that is now emerging is this: any goal-directed action is instigated by a central motivational state, which itself is created by an interaction within the brain between the neural consequences of bodily organismic states ("drives") and neural consequences of environmental incentives ("reinforcers"). Changes in behaviour that have traditionally been produced by manipulating "motivation" or "reinforcement" are the outcomes of influences from both the bodily organismic states and the environmental incentive objects.' Nothing in this descriptive account would lead one to suspect that motivation implies conflict, for it remains on the level of mechanisms and ignores experience.

Another related difference from psychoanalytic dynamics is the implicit assumption that the 'how' of motivation is the crucial question, rather than the 'what'. Freud's dynamics is continuously concerned with the content of the psychological representations which instinctual drives acquire, with the semantics rather than the mechanics of conflict.

The temptations of physiology are, of course, considerable for many psychologists; not only because of the inherent fascination of the subject; not only because of the attractions of reductionism, but above all because body and mind are experientially indeed inseparable. Freud, too, was of course not averse to physiology. Nowhere does this become clearer than in the elaboration of what he termed the economic point of view. It is as if he had asked himself: how can human behaviour and experience be most parsimoniously described and understood? and had assumed that the answer required a mechanistic stance, a search for processes which avoid the unending complexities of meaning. The economic point of view presents Freud's attempt at a reductionist psychology.

Basically, his answer came in terms of a postulated psychic energy of which everybody possesses a large but limited quantity which can be invested in or withdrawn from ideas, objects and various functions of the living organism. The earliest formulations of the nature of this energy occurred in *Project for a Scientific Psychology* and were clearly neurological, even though he emphasised later that he meant *psychic* energy. Yet the physiologically tinged language remained and must have been important for Freud's self-image as a natural scientist. He insisted that psychic energy was measurable in principle, even though appropriate measuring techniques had not yet been invented.

Laplanche and Pontalis[20] enumerate a number of clinical observations which cry out for a language of psychic energy: 'the irrepressible nature of the neurotic symptoms (often voiced by the patient in such expressions as "There was something in me that was stronger than me"); the triggering-off of troubles of a neurotic kind following disturbances of sexual discharge . . .', etc. There is a parallel to this in the ineradicable notion of psychic energy in common-sense psychology. We speak of people needing or finding outlets for their energy or concentrating it on one area at the expense of others; when a child seems to have lost his zest we assume that his energy is invested in some secret preoccupation, etc. The need for a systematic approach to the circulation and distribution of psychic energy seems imperative. That neither Freud, let alone common-sense psychology specify the nature of this energy need not bother us; they are in respectable company, for neither do physicists pronounce on the ultimate nature of gravity or electricity, but are content with describing and measuring their consequences. Freud was quite explicit on this point: 'we know nothing of the nature of the excitatory process . . . we do not feel justified in framing any hypothesis on the subject. We are consequently operating all the time with a large unknown factor, which we are obliged to carry over into every new formula.'[21]

In clinical descriptions Freud uses his energy language largely as a shorthand device. Take, for example, his summing up of the case history of the Wolfman: after having in some ten pages highlighted significant episodes and details, the patient's sexual development characterised by conflicting homosexual and heterosexual tendencies, etc., he sums up this mass of material in half a sentence of energy language thus: . . . his power of maintaining simultaneously the most various and contradictory libidinal cathexes, all of them capable of functioning side by side'.[22]

The trouble with the economic point of view lies not in its descriptive language; indeed its simplifications may be an important heuristic device for recognising similarities in apparently widely differing case histories, as long as it is recognised that there is a difference between a summary and an explanation. The difficulties arise because under the economic point of view Freud fell into the trap of extreme reductionism: seeking for the ultimate explanation, the principle under which all psychological phenomena could be subsumed. To begin with it was tension-reduction which served as his ultimate answer. Freud referred to the constancy principle which implies that the 'aim' of the organism is to keep the quantity of excitation in itself at as low a level as possible, or at any rate constant, and he equated this with the pleasure principle, that is with the avoidance of unpleasure. But he was too good a clinician to leave matters at that. It did not escape his notice that increasing tension could be experienced as pleasurable and be sought after rather than avoided; nor that sexual energy—libido—was qualitatively so different from the energy involved in self-preservation that no common denominator could adequately account for the manifestations of either. He recognised that there was not a simple co-ordination between the constancy and the pleasure principle but neither clarified the issue nor abandoned it. Clinical observations compelled him to couple with the pleasure principle the reality principle capable of modifying the former by converting free into bound energy, a duality which corresponds to primary and secondary processes. Late in his work yet another duality takes over, the life and death instincts with their specific energies, and the ultimate triumph of the nirvana principle, the reduction of tension to zero in the death of the organism.[23]

The inconsistencies and contradictions in Freud's reductionist economic speculations have exercised the minds of friend and foe, while some psychoanalysts continue to use the language of the economic point of view as if it presented an explanation of the clinical data.

Two comments on Freud's economic metapsychology, one stemming from an experimental psychologist who was also a psychoanalyst, and the other from a philosopher, both deeply immersed in Freudian thought, are worth mentioning in detail because the former presents so clear a formulation of incompatibilities in Freud's thought, the latter because it suggests a limit to the realm of discourse within which psychoanalytic thought is valid.

George Klein[24] wrote an essay under the title 'Freud's Two Theories of Sexuality' in which he said: 'There is reason to believe that the psychoanalytic conception of sexuality occurs in two versions. The first I will call the clinical theory because it is the one that tacitly guides actual clinical work. It centres on the distinctive properties of human sexual experience, on the values and meanings associated with sensual experience . . . The second version translates this psychological conception to the quasi-physiological terms of a model of an energic force that "seeks" discharge. This energic conception is connected with Freud's fundamental belief . . . .: that the source of all activity in the organism . . . is its tendency to deal with the energic influxes of "stimuli", to discharge them, and to reduce the tensions of their quantity.' Klein goes on to say that 'the two theories are on different logical planes, are not reducible one to the other, and require different data for confirmation; they are in critical ways even inconsistent with each other'.

The relation between meaning and mechanisms implied in that passage is actually the central theme of Ricoeur's remarkable book on Freud: 'Desire' is his term for Freud's libido. 'The language of desire', he says, 'is a discourse combining meaning and force.'[25] He regards desire as the 'concept at the frontier between the organic and the psychical',[26] which limits the realm beyond which psychoanalysis cannot proceed, for in his view it is not a natural science but hermeneutics, that is a systematic effort to disentangle the logic of double or ambiguous meaning. For this reason Ricoeur believes that psychoanalysis can never be blended into psychology which he classifies as a natural science.

Whether psychology, however, even in its most rigorous natural science stance, can ever successfully avoid the problem of meaning in the long run is another question. For decades tension reduction was also regarded as a fundamental principle of large areas of academic psychology; not only in animal psychology where it still carries the major burden as an explanation of behaviour but even in social psychology where the recently fashionable theory of cognitive dissonance[27] was based on the principle of tension reduction, in agreement, as it were, with the pleasure but not the reality principle. But tension reduction as the fundamental mechanism of behaviour has run into difficulties also in academic psychology. All manner of new drives had to be postulated in order to fit observed behaviour into the procrustean bed of tension reduction: exploratory behaviour in animals reduced the tension created by a curiosity drive; change of preferences or opinions reduced the tension created by a drive towards cognitive consistency. Academic psychology as much as Freud's economic metapsychology leave the problem of whether it is possible to translate meaning into mechanism, and how this could be done, equally unsolved. Ricoeur solves the problem for psychoanalysis by restricting it to the study of 'the semantics of desire'—the interpretation of meaning only. But by the same token it assigns to academic psychology a task which it has valiantly pursued yet discovered to be unmanageable: the restriction to mechanisms only.

It is fortunately easier to describe Freud's topographic point of view, particularly if one ignores—as I intend to—the occasional intrusion in his writings of economic concepts into other points of view. The basic question here arose already in Freud's contact with the French hypnotists and in his collaboration with Breuer: to what extent does man know the reasons for his own actions and feelings? His patients convinced him of the most general answer—to a very small extent. They could not explain why, for example, they could not fall asleep without first engaging in a certain ritual, or why they felt unhappy and unfulfilled, let alone why rational argument was powerless against some irrational fears such as the Ratman's horrifying torture phantasy or, in extreme disturbances such as in the Schreber case, why he mistook phantasy for reality when he maintained that he was a girl frightened of indecent assault or a woman impregnated by God.[28] The formalised answer and its elaboration extended Freud's thought beyond his patients into general psychology. The concept of three different stages of consciousness—the unconscious, the pre-conscious and the conscious—Freud's notions about which part of mental life occurs at which stage and why, as much as the discussion of transition from one to another in both directions, are relevant to all human beings, not only the disturbed, even though they are, of course, central to psychoanalysis as a therapy.

To put the question which corresponds to the topographic point of view as has been done, namely as referring to the extent of unaided self-knowledge, brings into focus the status of introspection in the psychoanalytic method. It is a mistake to regard the psychoanalytic method as introspection,[29] certainly if introspection is regarded as a method which produces answers to psychological questions. Early in this century Titchener used introspection in this manner. He wanted to arrive at the elements of consciousness by training subjects exposed to a visual object to report not what they were seeing but how seeing was experienced within themselves, what it felt like to see. For the phenomenologists introspection is, of course, central: it provides the only psychological evidence they recognise. These uses of introspection, predicated upon an unconcern with unconscious mental life, or on its denial, regard the result of self-observation as valid by definition. Freud, too, uses self-observation; indeed, the basic rule of psychoanalysis is nothing if not a request for self-observation. But the result of this process are data which by themselves do not provide answers to the psychological problems which trouble the patient, even though their validity as data is accepted by the analyst. It requires the psychoanalytic dialogue to make sense out of this raw material which is fragmented and unsystematic, and is in its early stages certainly not experienced by either patient or analyst as 'answers'. The phenomenological approach has the undoubted advantage of relative simplicity; but it has no way of dealing with the many occasions where an introspective effort to arrive at an answer to, say, the question of why one is in a bad mood, or experiences intense fear and disgust at the sight of certain animals, yields the answer: I do not know. Psychoanalysis does not take 'no' for an answer. It aims to make sense of the unknown, perhaps the unknowable as Freud realised: 'We have discovered technical methods of filling up the gaps in the phenomena of our consciousness, and we make use of those methods just as a physicist makes use of experiment. In this manner we infer a number of processes which are in themselves "unknowable" and interpolate them in those that are conscious to us. And if, for instance, we say: "At this point something occurred of which we are totally unable to form a conception, but which, if it had entered our consciousness, could only have been described in such and such a way."'[30]

Sartre's critique of Freud could be summarised in his different answer to the topographic question: what man consciously knows about himself, he might say, is all there is to be known about him. He says: 'By rejecting the conscious unity of the psyche, Freud is obliged to imply everywhere a magic unity linking distant phenomena across obstacles, just as sympathetic magic unites the spellbound person and the wax image fashioned in his likeness.'[31] In the light of the previously quoted passage by Freud one wonders about the appropriateness of the magic analogy. The unity of personality is axiomatic for Freud, as has been pointed out before; the link between the assumed unconscious and the conscious is forged not by magic but by phenomena in consciousness which defy understanding unless they are regarded as consequences of matters which occur outside awareness.

The topographic question is also being asked by psychologists and tackled experimentally in the field of subliminal perception and in studies of hypnosis.[32] It remains to be seen whether phenomenologists can deal with the phenomena there discovered without the assumption of unconscious processes.

In a previous chapter Freud's answer to the topographic question was presented as his first theory of personality which became incorporated in his second, based on the structural point of view. Where metapsychology is understood as the basic assumptions of psychoanalysis, as in Rapaport's work, or as Freud's various non-parsimonious models of man, as in Hilgard's formulation, the topographical conception is regarded as superfluous and dropped from the general discussion. To be sure, Rapaport points out that while Freud never explicitly revoked the topographic point of view, he became impatient with it on occasions, and he quotes from *The Ego and the Id* to that effect: '. . . we land in endless confusion and difficulty if we cling to our former way of expressing ourselves and try, for instance, to derive neuroses from a conflict between the conscious and the unconscious. We shall have to substitute for this antithesis another, taken from our understanding of the structural conditions of the mind . . .'[33]

When, however, the metapsychological points of view are taken to indicate the basic psychological questions which preoccupied Freud, the topographical and the structural present distinct areas of curiosity, neither subsumed by the other. The question underlying the structural point of view is no longer the extent of possible self-knowledge but rather: what are the conceptual ingredients for a comprehensive description of personality? The question demands an answer in terms of structures, that is in terms of relatively enduring, habitual and slow changing patterns of behaving and experiencing. But beyond this formal requirement it achieves meaning through Freud's implicit, parsimonious and comprehensive categorisation of the three simultaneous psychological imperatives with which we live: to deal with our desires, with the real world and with out consciences. For each of these permanent tasks Freud introduces the 'fiction' of a mental apparatus, a structure in the sense defined before: the id, ego and super-ego. The degree of conflict or balance within and between these three habitual patterns constitute personality.

It should be noted that Freud's structural point of view implies universal categories, applicable to one and all, not a typology of personality. To be sure, he wrote occasionally of certain personality types—the 'anal' or 'oral' character, for example—but he was not interested in establishing a comprehensive typology; he suggested a conceptually comprehensive and basic scheme within which the infinite variety of actual personalities could be contained.

Hartmann[34] points out that the distinction between ego, id and super-ego resembles Aristotle's identification of the basic goals of human action as 'profit, pleasure, morality'. But it remained for Freud, from the structural point of view, to ask how it can come about that one or two of these goals can be sacrificed to the other, how all three can be in harmony or conflict—in a word, to achieve psychological understanding of a person.

Freud's answer to the structural question leads logically to the genetic point of view (*de facto* Freud's concern with developmental questions historically preceded the structural ideas). In a broad and unspecific sense concern with development is, perhaps, the most widely shared topic of interest among all psychologists. But the communality of interest should not hide the fact that concern with the past, in psychology as much as in history, can be implemented from different points of view. 'Whig history', we learn, is the study of the past from the point of view of the present; there is another approach to the study of history renouncing the idea of systematic progress in favour of establishing 'wie es denn eigentlich gewesen ist' (how it actually was). These two different approaches are particularly clear in the history of ideas and of science, where many books continue to trace a line of progress from past thought culminating inevitably in the ideas of the here and now. Thomas Kuhn's *Structure of Scientific Revolutions*[35] has undermined this approach; in an even more radical fashion Foucault[36] has reconstructed the climate of thought in past centuries 'wie es denn eigentlich gewesen ist', and denied the existence of a systematic link between the changing 'epistemes' (his word for the basic intellectual assumptions common to all sciences in one era).

Freud started off as a Whig historian, as it were, but had to learn the hard way about the danger inherent in this approach of falsifying the past. The crucial event was of course his first seduction theory. From the present conditions of his patients, a traumatic actual seduction in childhood made sense. But was it actually so? Whig history is a selective constructionist view of the past, accepting what appears to lead in an unbroken line to the present and ignoring events which do not help us to understand the here and now. Freud, as we know, rejected actual early seduction because of its sheer implausibility as the earliest origin of neuroses, notwithstanding its explanatory power. He began to ask himself how the child had to experience himself and the world around him, as a question in its own right, independent of what he knew about a person's present situation. Ideally, one would want to know both: how matters actually were at each stage of development and why certain constellations influenced the next stage while others did not. Freud did not achieve this ideal position, but he recognised that the way to it lay in a combination of prospective and retrospective approaches. In the *Three Essays* he expressed the view that a combination of direct child observation with psychoanalysis would yield more satisfactory results.[37]

Freud himself elaborated genetic propositions only with regard to the sexual drives and in particular with regard to the inevitability of conflict in that sphere. The issue bears, of course, on the nature/nurture controversy, on the relative power of maturational versus experiential aspects of development. While Freud has been misrepresented as concentrating on the maturation of instinctual drives, his general position was clearly interactionist: 'The constitutional factor must await experiences before it can make itself felt; the accidental factor must have a constitutional basis in order to come into operation.'[38]

In the genetic point of view the concept of regression in

time has a central role. That people revert under certain conditions, particularly when under stress, to earlier patterns of behaviour is now widely accepted as a phenomenon. To make regression as a process understandable it is necessary to assume that past experience and behaviour is not 'lost', even though it may escape conscious memory, but is somehow available to an individual. Freud's general claim that nothing is lost must be understood as meaning that nothing that was ever psychologically relevant is lost and is, at least potentially, available to consciousness. It is hard, if not impossible, to explain the phenomenon of regression by any other set of assumptions. Yet, Freud's genetic approach which implies these assumptions has been criticised as overrating the impact of the past on present psychological states and underrating the acquisition of new patterns.[39] As Hartmann[40] has pointed out, this amounts to wrongly equating continuity with the past as identity with it, while Freud recognised that development did not just consist in the preservation of infantile tendencies but in the formation of new patterns, thus integrating the genetic point of view with the structural one. Early development leads to early structures capable of functions which were outside the repertoire of the individual before the structure was formed. 'Functional autonomy', as Allport termed the acquisition of new patterns of behaving and experiencing, is not incompatible with psychoanalysis.

It would be wrong, however, to conclude that the implications of the genetic point of view are all consistent with other psychoanalytic assumptions. The compulsion to repeat is a phenomenon which Freud identified in the play of children, in the transference situation and in neurotic symptoms. The effort to assign the phenomenon to a proper conceptual place, however, led Freud not only to restricting his earlier asserted power of the pleasure principle—repeating painful or traumatic events cannot conceivably be subsumed under the pleasure principle—but to inconsistencies and intellectual dilemmas.

Finally, it has been suggested by Rapaport that the metapsychology implies a distinct adaptive point of view, which he defines as follows: 'The adaptive point of view demands that the psychoanalytic explanation of any psychological phenomenon include propositions concerning its relationship to the environment'.[41] In his clinical and theoretical writings Freud is invariably concerned with psychological functioning in the real world. It is, of course, the starting point for every individual analysis, and basic concepts such as primary and secondary processes, pleasure and reality principle, the ego functions, etc., clearly indicate that he was continuously concerned with the impact of the environment. But his notions about the relation between man and the world around him underwent several changes as Rapaport has elsewhere demonstrated.[42]

At first his concern was with the role of reality in understanding his patients' symptoms and feelings. Reality was then the enemy interfering with the instinctual drives, against which a person defended himself as best he could. His second conception of reality was based on the recognition that instinctual drives needed real objects for discharge, and that human beings, in contrast to animals, can make choices and substitutions between objects to satisfy certain of their basic needs; this implied the ability to discriminate between such objects through reality testing by secondary thought processes. In contrast to the earlier conception pleasure and reality principles here do not work against each other; adaptation to reality acquired a positive survival function. In a third stage Freud acknowledged that external reality had a motivating power. The ego is now regarded as capable of objectivity with regard to reality; it is indeed largely shaped by it. When Freud wrote in *Civilization and Its Discontents*[43] that 'work is man's strongest tie to reality' he clearly meant that adaptation to reality is essential for individual survival.

While he nowhere elaborated his notions on adaptation systematically, while earlier connotations of his views on reality coloured later ones and while therefore some confusion remained, it is under the adaptive point of view that his basic outlook on the condition of man found expression in *The Future of an Illusion*[44] and *Civilization and Its Discontents*.[45]

This presentation of the metapsychological points of view started with the assumption that the body of thought Freud presented under these terms cannot possibly be regarded as a coherent theory and the exposition should have made it clear why the assumption was made in the first place; the suggestion was that metapsychology is Freud's agenda for a general human psychology. What does this agenda look like when divested of Freud's own terminology? The following major topics emerge: the dynamics of conflict; the limitations of self-knowledge; the reducibility of meaning to mechanism; personality; development; and relation to the environment. As fundamental questions within a general psychology these points of view form an impressive agenda as urgent now as it was in Freud's time. The dilemma and the challenge of psychoanalytic thought lie in Freud's recognition that these fundamental questions lead to ideas, assumptions and speculations which sometimes overlap while at others they are mutually inconsistent. And yet he required them to be simultaneously applied. The metapsychology was aimed at the Herculean task of theoretical linkage, even though it was in the end performed more in the style of Sisyphus.

CHAPTER 7

In Search of Validation

CRITICS, doubtful of the validity of psychoanalysis, have created the impression that Freud simply and arrogantly asserted the truth content of his statements without bothering to consider the all important problem of validity. Nothing could be further from the facts. That Freud was capable of arrogance *vis-à-vis* some of his colleagues seems well established.[1] But arrogance as the personal quality of a man who did not live among his equals in intellectual power is really neither here nor there, even if one took a psychoanalytic stance and interpreted such a personal attribute as an indication of uncertainty. For there is more obvious, direct and indirect, evidence in Freud's writings of a passionate desire to discover ways in which the validity of psychoanalytic findings could be established. Indeed, it is no exaggeration to say that the search for validation pervaded his entire work, that he knew or anticipated every form of criticism which can be raised against psychoanalysis and that he tried to deal with them as best he could, sometimes to his own satisfaction, sometimes not.

There are three major aspects of Freud's writings which demonstrate this concern: direct statements about the validity of interpretations and constructions in psychoanalysis as a therapy; aspects of his style of presentation; and his excursions into other human sciences.

From the days of his involvement with hypnosis Freud was fully aware of the power of suggestion, a term which he dismissed, however, later on since it merely suggested a word to fill the gap in knowledge of how hypnosis worked. But once the psychoanalytic procedure was established, the question arose of whether what patients reported in their associations was actually their own production or the result of suggestion or even leading questions by the analyst.

Freud was too sensitive and honest an observer to deny this possibility outright. Indeed, in his 'Remarks on the Theory and Practice of Dream Interpretation'[2] Freud states that the manifest content of dreams of analysands is indeed influenced by the analytic situation, but he maintains that the latent dream thought is outside the suggestive power of the analyst. In other words, the analytic hour which is for most people a powerful experience which, in addition, has the character of an uncompleted task, presents a particularly potent day residue on which a dream may concentrate. The power of the day residue in shaping the manifest content of dreams had actually been demonstrated empirically already in 1917 by Pötzl.[3] But since the manifest dream content is in itself not important and only the occasion, like other memories and free associations of the patient, for arriving at psychoanalytic findings through interpretation and constructions, the question of validity and of the power of suggestion is most serious for these procedures employed by the analyst in the analytic dialogue. Throughout his work from the beginning to the end Freud struggled with the problem that the patient's associations themselves could be provoked by the analyst's interpretations or constructions: that the analysand produced what he sensed the analyst wanted to hear. Freud[4] introduced rules for the analyst's assessment of the validity of his own interpretations (i.e. the ascription of meaning to a relatively isolated event, action or free association) and constructions (i.e. the reconstitution of a forgotten part of the patient's childhood situation) which were designed to eliminate compliance as well as resistance as faulty criteria for either validation or invalidation of the psychoanalyst's contributions to the dialogue: the patient's agreement or disagreement must by itself not be taken on face value. A 'yes' to an interpretation may only indicate positive transference to the analyst, a 'no' negative transference or resistance to accepting the implications of an interpretation. The analyst should infer that he is wrong in his search for understanding when his interpretation or construction produces no reaction in the patient, not even a denial; he should conclude that more material is required before offering a new interpretation or construction. By the same token he can assume to be on the right track if the patient builds the offered interpretation into further associations. A typical phrase by which patients deal with a correct interpretation and which recurs in many analyses is: 'I never thought of it that way but . . .' followed by new material fitting into the emerging pattern of the jig-saw puzzle.

In the Wolfman case Freud offered towards the end of the analysis a construction which demonstrated the working of this rule: the Wolfman, at the age of about eighteen months, must have observed intercourse between his parents *a tergo* and must have been frightened by the experience. This construction led indeed to further associations and to an understanding of the events and emotions of the Wolfman's early childhood which made sense to him and made possible the end of the analysis for the time being (he returned to analysis years later). But Freud was not yet convinced: 'Out of critical interest I made one more attempt to force upon the patient another view of his story, which might commend itself more to sober common sense . . . his observation of intercourse, I argued, was a phantasy of his later years . . . but the patient looked at me uncomprehendingly and a little contemptuously when I put this view before him, and he never reacted to it again.' But only two pages further on in the case history Freud wrote: 'I would myself be glad to know whether the primal scene in my present patient's case was a phantasy or a real experience.'[5] His own doubts were hard to appease. But there is contained in this rule for validating psychoanalysis as a technique an idea which is familiar to psychologists and social scientists under the term convergent validity. No skilled analyst would ever venture a construction unless it was suggested in different contexts with different material from different sessions which were on the surface unrelated to each other but converged on the same underlying meaning. In academic psychology, which has, of course, also to deal with inferences on underlying processes which cannot be directly observed (for example, in the study of attitudes), converging validity is obtained by the application of a variety of methods, sampling the inferred attitude from differently elicited responses.[6]

Validation by independent verification of childhood events impressed Freud on various occasions. He reports that a childhood event in the life of one of his early patients could be confirmed from the diary her mother had kept in those days.[7] In understanding his own dreams he checked with his mother and discovered, for example, that in his childhood the Freud family was attended by a one-eyed doctor whom Freud had connected in his dream with a schoolmaster. Important though such factual validation is, it has of course no direct bearing on the validity of the theory into which such facts fit.

In the introduction to the case study of Little Hans, Freud urged his students to engage in direct observation of children, and he obviously took Hans' father's reports as welcome examples of such direct observation.[8] In the Ratman case Freud discusses the difficulty of establishing the historical truth of an early memory which may be a sexualised reconstruction of what actually happened but also mentions the verification of a childhood episode.[9]

As a rule, however, external validation was not available and Freud had to rely on the previously described rule of internal converging validation. Ideally, Freud thought, constructions would be fully validated if they led the patient to recall his forgotten childhood in an unbroken chain of detailed episodes which confirmed the analyst's guess. In practice this was unachievable.

But even if Freud as a therapist was prepared to settle for less than complete reconstruction of a psychological life history, even though he recognised that not every dream was interpretable or that a dream could have several interpretations, his patients presented him within these realistic limits with other reasons for doubt and uncertainty. Take, for example, the case of Dora: Freud proposed to her a construction of an earlier event in her life which this intelligent girl accepted as intellectually plausible; but she steadfastly insisted that nothing in her memory corroborated Freud's construction.[10] Freud himself, always very explicit on his mistakes, thought he had been faulty in his handling of Dora's transference neurosis. But the particular incident of the unconfirmed construction recalls a question he had asked himself and left unanswered even earlier in the *Studies on Hysteria*, where he had wondered whether it was possible that a patient's thought, made explicit during analysis, had only been potentially present in the past.

It is the same doubt that induced him to experiment by suggesting an alternative construction to the Wolfman, that led him to recommend direct childhood observations, that seems never to have left him, notwithstanding the many occasions on which the patient's response to the analyst's hypothesis formulated as a construction was confirmed by eliciting further material.

The question arises: does it matter whether the construction of the primal scene in the Wolfman case recaptured an actual event, a later phantasy of the patient or a plausible image in the mind of the analyst, as long as its presentation had the desired effect of producing a more coherent and meaningful self-image in the Wolfman? Freud faced the question but vacillated in his answer. In the context of expressing his own wish to know whether that primal scene had actually occurred, he adds: 'I must admit that the answer to this question is not in fact a matter of very great importance.' Yet in the seduction theory of neurosis and its abandonment the distinction between phantasy and reality had obviously been of major importance.

If it were a question of therapy only, perhaps the validation of a construction could be ignored. As Freud said, everything that helps is thereby legitimate; he even believed that psychoanalysis could not compete with Lourdes in number of cures.[11] But Freud was never a therapist only. What led him to develop the psychoanalytic technique and rely on it as the bedrock of all his work and thought was his scientific curiosity, his desire to understand through the data which the method elicited, data unique in quantity and quality, man's psychological condition. And from that point of view the establishment of validity was overwhelmingly important. Freud repeatedly insisted that concepts and theoretical formulations were open to revision, which he offered more and more tentatively with advancing age as the speculations of an old and tired man to be improved by those who followed him. It was the status of his data and observations that mattered most; how else could one choose between Freudian psychoanalysis and competing systems, such as Jung's or Adler's, for example?

How indeed? The question is central for assigning intellectual status to psychoanalysis and has, accordingly, preoccupied philosophers of science from the beginning of the century to the present day. Flew, for example, has suggested that the problem of validation presents 'peculiarities . . . such as to ensure that their central and basic place in psychoanalysis must give this discipline a logical status different from, though not of course for that reason either inferior or superior to, that of sciences concerned with things other than human beings, and even from that of sciences concerned with less distinctly human aspects of human beings.'[12]

Freud would not have agreed. One recalls his statement that psychoanalysis is a natural science, 'what else could it be?' But others have offered answers to this rhetorically meant question, aligning psychoanalysis with hermeneutics, that is the interpretation of ambiguous meaning, foremost among them Ricoeur and Habermas.

Since Habermas[13] takes psychoanalysis as an outstanding example of a hermeneutic science emphasising the inseparability of method and theory, it is worth mentioning briefly what he regards as the 'data' for a hermeneutic discipline. There are three types: linguistic expression, which needs hermeneutics only when sender and receiver talk about different things in a common language; actions which express only part of their psychological context so that their intentions and purposes require interpretation; and experiential expressions such as gestures, physiognomy, laughing or crying. These are, of course, the types of data available to psychoanalysis. According to him a hermeneutic interpretation is valid to the extent that the interpretation of parts agrees with the interpretation of the whole configuration. This conception of validity is saved from becoming a fool's paradise in a viciously closed circle in psychoanalysis by the fact that it is arrived at through a dialogue. Unless the interpretation makes sense to *both*, the patient and the analyst, it lacks validity.

Notwithstanding Habermas' powerful arguments, there remains a problem about hermeneutic validity in the psychoanalytic situation. If an analysand has become very dependent on the psychoanalyst, it is conceivable that the dialogue is one in form only while in fact the analyst's interpretation of detail is governed by his own construction of complex events, the patient producing under the power of the transference neurosis the appropriate associations. That this amounts to a mishandling of the technique does, unfortunately, not preclude its occurrence. This inherent difficulty must have been in Freud's mind when he wrote to Pfister in a somewhat defeatist mood that analysis is best suited for the healthy, who do not really need it.

Psychoanalysis as hermeneutics belongs to the *Geisteswissenschaften*, for which the term humanistic sciences is the only available translation, even though not quite catching the connotation of the German term. Like history or literary criticism, psychoanalysis cannot, then, establish its validity in the manner of the natural sciences by prediction or postdiction from theory, but must rely above all on the coherence of part and whole interpretation, using converging evidence from 'factual' events if and when it can find it.

The question arises whether conventional natural science tests of validity are inoperative only for psychoanalysis or also for large segments of academic psychology, as Flew implies. A remarkable article by Cronbach,[14] one of the foremost quantitative methodologists in social psychology, suggests that there too the limits of experimental predictive validation are now being recognised. He advocates 'intensive local observation [which] goes beyond discipline to an open-eyed, open-minded appreciation of the surprises nature deposits in the investigative net. This kind of interpretation is historical more than scientific. I suspect that if the psychologist were to read more widely in history, ethnology, and the centuries of humanistic writings on man and society, he would be better prepared for this part of his work.'

That Freud anticipated Cronbach's advice about reading is well known, even if he did not abide by Cronbach's warning against seeking for timeless theories about the nature of man, also contained in that article. To the extent that his unceasing search for validation was expressed in his style, he was very far from claiming a special logical status for psychoanalysis. On the contrary. As a rule he took the arguments against his work in the stance of a natural science debate, undermining their logical coherence[15] where possible, providing evidence from his clinical work where he could[16] and referring to other people's work much more than his critics give him credit for.[17] But beyond these customary forms of academic debate Freud's style has characteristics which I take as evidence for the extent of his uncertainty, the need to persuade himself as much as the rest of the world. A very large proportion of his writings is argument, counter-argument and self-criticism, rather than straight exposition. The *Introductory* and *New Introductory Lectures* are appropriate examples. Take Lecture 31, 'Dissection of the Psychical Personality':[18] early on Freud deals with the objection to psychoanalysis 'that human beings are not merely sexual creatures but have nobler and higher impulses as well', which he counters by saying that 'even psychoanalysis was not able to study every field simultaneously', but was now ready for ego psychology and the super-ego. A little later he anticipates that the introduction of these terms will lead to the scornful accusation that psychoanalytic ego-psychology 'comes down to nothing more than taking commonly used abstractions literally and in a crude sense, and transforming them from concepts into things'. He advises his audience to 'hold your contemptuous criticism for the time being . . .' A few pages further on he apologises for not being able to explain the super-ego formulation better, but 'we ourselves' do not feel sure that we understand it completely . . .' and 'I myself am far from satisfied with these remarks . . .' He anticipates Marxist criticism of the power of the super-ego in understanding social behaviour: 'materialistic views of history . . . brush it [the super-ego] aside with the remark that human ideologies are nothing other than the product and superstructure of their contemporary economic conditions. That is true, but very probably not the whole truth . . .' Talking of the timeless nature of the repressed he self-critically says that he has made little progress in dealing with this idea. Toward the end of the lecture he emphasises again the tentativeness of his theorising: 'You must not judge too harshly a first attempt at giving a pictorial representation of something so intangible as psychical processes.'

The Question of Lay Analysis[19] is written as a dialogue with a benevolent and unbiased imaginary critic of psychoanalysis, discussing and refuting many of the then current criticisms.

There are many other examples demonstrating his full awareness of criticisms of psychoanalysis as much as his own unceasing preoccupation with them. But there is yet another feature of his style which I take as evidence of his search for validity, namely his argumentation with himself. Freud's style has received much praise, not only in the award of the Goethe prize. If one takes as an attribute of good style the inevitable losses suffered in translation, Freud certainly scores high, notwithstanding the scholarly excellence of Strachey's translation in the *Standard Edition*. To give just one example, Rycroft[20] draws attention to the connotation of existential terror in the German term *Angst*. In English anxiety is rather a harmless or even a beneficial affair. The emphasis on Freud's good style and readability thanks to the richness of his imagery, the use of analogies and—in German —his relative freedom from professional jargon, disguises, however, a genuine difficulty in reading Freud, whether in the original or in translation. The sentences may be easy to grasp, but the underlying structure of thought is complex and difficult to take in. The reader must be prepared to take

a long breath and hold his horses to the very end of an essay
before being in a position to know what Freud said. As a rule
he does not set out just to communicate the result of his
thought processes, but these processes themselves as they led
him to an always tentative conclusion. As a result one page
or paragraph is changed or qualified in a later one. In
between there are splendid aphoristic formulations which
convey to the reader an 'Ah, ha' experience of understanding,
though he may have to be prepared to correct a too early
sense of closure.

On the other hand, Freud often introduces new concepts
with appropriate qualifications but then continues to use
them in shorthand manner without repeating the qualifications. In an essay 'On Transformations of Instincts as
Exemplified in Anal Erotism'[21] this sentence about neurotic
women appears: 'we not infrequently meet with the repressed
wish to possess a penis'; later penis envy is given conceptual
status in the theory as if it were a universal phenomenon,
implying greater theoretical certainty than he felt according
to his own often repeated statements to that effect.

The expression of doubt, the anticipation of criticism and
its refutation, the preference for argument and counter-
argument, the presentation of the development of thought—
all these aspects of Freud's style convey the impression of a
mind driven by passionate curiosity to discoveries and formulations which he himself felt were disturbing and original,
and which needed continuous efforts at validation. Late in
life, in 'Analysis Terminable and Interminable'[22] Freud expressed his sense of being almost overwhelmed by his own
thoughts when he confessed an occasional 'doubt whether
the dragons of primaeval ages are really extinct'. In this
situation of a turmoil of ideas and their implications which
he felt 'too old and sick' to disentangle to his own satisfaction,
Freud consciously and deliberately held on to clinical data
as both the origin and the justification of his entire work.
Certainly nobody before Freud had ever amassed a comparable amount of details for an individual case. While he
knew that 'naturally a single case does not give us all the

information that we should like to have', he added: 'Or, to put it more correctly, it might teach us everything, if we were only in a position to make everything out, and if we were not compelled by the inexperience of our own perception to content ourselves with a little.'[23]

Apart from demonstrating, once again, a characteristic feature of Freud's style—the first sentence out of context could easily be used as an advocacy of statistical research, the second views the single case study as containing in principle the answers to all questions about the human condition—these views show why Freud made himself into an unsurpassed master in attention to detail.

Parenthetically it may be noted that Freud's habitual thought pattern of going from a minute detail to a high-level abstraction and back again to detail demonstrates the operation of a form of intelligence which has so far escaped the attention of intelligence testers as well as Piagetian thought about intelligence which regards it as the ability to stand back from one's immediate sense perceptions. Both views, supported by the practices in higher education, identify the level of intelligence with the level of abstraction. The omission of the last step—the ability to return from abstraction to concrete detail—exemplified by Freud, prevents the usual methods of research on intelligence from becoming relevant to problem-solving.

In any case, attention to detail also marks Freud's excursions into fields outside the clinical situation. Take as a first example Freud's beautiful and revealing essay 'The Moses of Michelangelo'.[24] Freud was deeply moved when he first saw the statue in Rome and returned repeatedly to it. The essay first reviews what various art historians have said about it. Most of them have argued that Michelangelo showed Moses who holds the Tables of the Ten Commandments at the moment when he returned from Mount Sinai and surprised his people in the dance around the golden calf. Freud argues against this interpretation; there is no anger, contempt or pain in Moses' face; Moses rests and does not appear at the point of springing to his feet. Freud then notes two details, overlooked by the art historians, the attitude of his right hand and the position of the Tables. From these details Freud concludes that Michelangelo aimed to transform the traditional hot-tempered Moses into one who transcends his passion into a state of calm and sublimation. The essay closes in this manner: 'What if this interpretation is wrong? I cannot tell.' Doubt, once again. Yet the Michelangelo essay meets *mutatis mutandis* the clinical validation rule: it makes sense of more details than alternative interpretations. One might even be tempted to say that it applies the clinical validation rule to a non-clinical situation. Being well aware of the unique nature of the psychoanalytic situation, Freud sought validity for what he had there discovered in other fields which were clearly independent of the relation between an analyst and his patient, in history, philosophy, literature, art, anthropology and religion.

Freud was not a polymath in the technical sense, notwithstanding his wide and varied reading. He was a psychologist above all and single-mindedly so; a hedgehog, not a fox in Isaiah Berlin's[25] memorable image of the two distinct types of creative mind based on a fragmentary poetic text from antiquity: the fox knows many things, but the hedgehog knows one big thing. The one thing that Freud knew, the psychological condition of man, he wanted to validate by all available means, including the enduring creations of the human mind. Freud argued implicitly that if what he knew was valid, then it must manifest itself somehow in the 'objective' social, historical and artistic achievements of mankind. The argument recalls Karl Bühler's all too neglected view that psychology should use man-made objects for inference on the maker. Of course the nature of such 'objective' results of the human psyche holds its own intrinsic fascination which Freud must have experienced too, as his collection of antiquities testifies. But when he wrote about art and artists, man, society and its history outside his theoretical and clinical work, he wrote as a psychologist in search of validation. He said as much in his preface to Reik's *Ritual*: 'psychoanalysis enters other mental sciences [Geisteswissenschaften in German] in order to test psychoanalytic ideas'.[26]

To read Freud's essay on Dostoevsky as literary criticism or as biographical research is as foolish as reading *Totem and Taboo* as anthropology. In both cases Freud was, of course, completely dependent on then available secondary sources. These works ought to be read as documents for Freud's search for validation in elaborating the implications of his psychological thought; then what he says makes powerful sense indeed. But the question is: can these writings be accepted as validations?

Here the situation becomes complicated. For in both the instances mentioned advanced scholarship has now thrown doubts on some of the biographical and anthropological facts on which Freud relied.

In the case of *Totem and Taboo*[27] Freud says he was stimulated by Wundt's *Völkerpsychologie* and Jung's work. His anthropological knowledge was taken largely from Frazer. He acknowledged his own deficiencies in the field and said that he entered it in order to create interest in the application of psychoanalytic thought to anthropological data. On the basis of the material available to him, Freud develops the parallelism between neurotic symptoms and primitive ritual, on the assumption that what has become unconscious in Western man was expressed in explicit rules in primitive societies. He draws attention, for example, to the dominance of ambivalence in symptoms and taboos. Taboos designate their object as both sacred and dangerous, as superior to the normal but also as unclean. Like neurotic symptoms they have no apparent motive, and they lead to ceremonial acts. Freud says early on that his assumptions about the origin of taboos are not verifiable,[28] but the parallel between symptoms and rituals is. Now, however inaccurate some of Frazer's anthropological descriptions may have been proved to be, these correspondences have not been questioned. Of course, Freud's fertile mind was not satisfied with establishing these similarities. He proceeded to speculate about their historical origin, and the myth of the primal horde and the killing of father was the result. This line of speculative investigation of historical and prehistorical phenomena, based on data provided by other scholars, culminated in *Moses and Monotheism*,[29] a work which shows the Sherlock Holmes quality of Freud's mind in most spectacular fashion. Central to the Moses book is the assumption that Moses was killed at the hand of his own people. Freud quotes a historian, Ernst Sellin, who in 1922 found 'unmistakable traces of a tradition' to that effect. Perhaps mankind will never know whether Moses did indeed meet a violent death. 'Unmistakable traces of a tradition' are certainly not final proof, even though it is important to underline that this assumption did not originate in Freud's work but in that of an historian's work. But the question of historical truth is almost beside the point of specifying what these works mean for psychoanalysis. Freud did not set himself the task of writing history. In his search for validation it is as if he had argued thus: if my clinical observations and the psychological theories to which they led have validity, then it must be possible to demonstrate that they help to illuminate completely different phenomena which share with my data only one fact: they are all creations of the human mind. Those prepared to accept converging validity and the hermeneutic notion that validity is established when the interpretation of the whole fits the interpretation of details, provided that such confirmatory details originate elsewhere—in the patient's mind or in historical documents—will grant that Freud's excursions into other human sciences have made a case for the validity of psychoanalysis. And yet—doubt persisted in his mind. As it does in ours.

CHAPTER 8

Freud's Heritage

FREUD was both an inheritor and an originator. Indeed it is doubtful whether, in the history of ideas which have made an impact comparable to those of Freud's, any other position is conceivable. Had there been no tradition of thought into which Freud's ideas fitted, he could hardly have conceived them; and even if he could they would not have survived. In his brilliant book *The Unconscious Before Freud* Whyte regards 'the continuity of the tradition of human thought and the productive imagination of individuals . . . [as] inseparable features of a single story'.[1] The reader should be forewarned that the following selective summary of that single story as others have traced it will make one question loom large: what, then, has Freud contributed? I shall try to answer it at the end of this chapter.

In his early psychoanalytic writings, particularly in *The Interpretation of Dreams*, Freud quoted his sources liberally and in the customary academic style, pointing out where he built on his predecessors, and where he disagreed with them. In the middle period of his working life references are quite rare; in his late writings on civilisation, religion and monotheism he carefully listed sources from other disciplines from which he had taken data for analysis and interpretation. In an article entitled 'A Note on the Prehistory of the Technique of Analysis'[2] Freud mentions three predecessors who had recognised the power of free association for self-discovery: in his correspondence with the poet Körner in 1788, Schiller recommended free association as the way to creative writing. In 1857 a Dr. J. J. Garth Wilkinson published a volume of verse which, he claimed, was produced by choosing a theme and then writing down whatever came to mind in relation to it. And the writer L. Börne, of whom Freud had been very fond as a schoolboy, advocated in 1823 that those who wished to produce novels should isolate themselves for three days and write down without hypocrisy and falsehood all that came to mind; he predicted they would be amazed at the originality of their own thoughts if they followed this prescription.

There is every reason to believe that Freud himself must have come across at least two of these statements many years before he wrote the article. Yet there he states that these statements had been drawn to his attention recently by friends or colleagues. Elsewhere Freud acknowledged what may apply to this article as well: a state of cryptomnesia, that is forgetting the source of an idea while remembering its content, and therefore experiencing it as one's own.

It is of some interest to note that experimental social psychologists have identified a similar phenomenon in studies of attitude change which they termed 'sleeper effect'.[3] They presented the opinion of a named expert on a public issue to their subjects; months later they ascertained their subjects' opinion on the same issue. While many of them had forgotten the original name, their own attitudes had shifted in the direction of his advocacy. The experimenters contented themselves with the identification of the phenomenon, leaving open the question of why memory should function in this peculiar fashion, retaining relatively complex ideas but forgetting a short and simple name. The Freudian model of the mind[4] with its assumption of meaningful associative links between nodal points suggests that while pre-existing associative connections could incorporate the content of the message, no such links were available for the name. If this interpretation of the experimentally produced sleeper effect is correct, it stands to reason that those deeply involved with ideas will manifest cryptomnesia more often than persons less so involved. Whyte even suggests that this unconscious memory for the ideas of others is a requirement for creative thought when he says: 'For Freud to achieve what he did . . . two conditions were necessary: that a long preparation should already have taken place and that he should himself be largely unaware of it, so that while unconsciously influenced by it he was free to make his own inferences from clinical observations.'[5]

Freud's heritage can be viewed in two ways: one can either focus on the mind of the man by tracing direct influences on his development, whether they were consciously remembered by him or were in St. Augustine's phrase 'forgotten memories'; or one can focus on the history of ideas which created in other minds a climate of thought receptive to what he had to say. Much of value for an understanding of Freud has emerged from the application of the first approach,[6] but it is unfortunately sometimes shrouded in controversy about the intellectual honesty of Freud, the man. A case in point is Maria Dorer's book,[7] in 1932 a relatively early contribution to Freud scholarship, in which she documents the similarity between Freud's and Herbart's dynamics, Herbart's concept of unconscious thought and his use of the term repression; she also accuses Freud of not having fully acknowledged his intellectual indebtedness to his teacher Meynert, who was himself influenced by Herbart. Freud expressed his indebtedness to Meynert in general terms: 'the great Meynert in whose footsteps I have trodden with such deep veneration', but he did not acknowledge any specific idea.

The emphasis here, however, will largely be on the second approach in an effort to highlight the uniqueness of the controversy over Freud: many before him have had similar ideas without arousing either the hostility or the adulation which Freud's thoughts aroused.

The history of thought throughout the centuries and the history of approaches to neurotic phenomena reveal a long chain of predecessors far beyond the three examples given by Freud. Notwithstanding the excellence of the two most outstanding works in this area—Whyte's, and Ellenberger's *The Discovery of the Unconscious*—there can be little doubt that further work, even if the search remains restricted to European ideas, will uncover additional material, demonstrating that virtually every single idea of Freud's had been conceived by somebody else before him.

No comprehensive treatment of available knowledge is intended here; a few examples must suffice to illustrate the long history of three fundamental ideas in psychoanalysis: the unconscious, the approach to treatment and understanding of emotional disorders, and infantile sexuality.

Whyte begins his examination with Descartes' dualism which he regards as a turning point in European self-awareness. Only after 'cogito ergo sum' had separated mind and matter was there a challenge to correct this creative error by questioning awareness as the essence of psychological processes. The Oxford dictionary gives 1697 as the date when the term self-conscious came into usage in the sense of being reflectively aware of one's identity, actions and sensations. It took more than a century, until 1837, for the term to acquire its negatively tinged connotation of morbid preoccupation with one's self. In between these dates Cartesian static rationalism (which, however, did not prevent Descartes from interpreting his own dreams, albeit not in a Freudian fashion, nor from explaining his preference for cock-eyed women by reference to a childhood experience) was increasingly challenged by ideas of change, transformations and an attack on consciousness as the defining characteristic of mental life. As Whyte says, 'the idea of unconscious mental processes was, in many of its aspects, conceivable around 1700, topical around 1800, and became effective around 1900 . . .',[8] even though he quotes some remarkable examples from much earlier periods (Galen, St. Augustine, Paracelsus, etc.).

Ralph Cudworth (1617–1688),[9] a Cambridge philosopher, wrote: 'It is certain, that our human souls themselves are not always conscious of whatever they have in them; for even the sleeping geometrician hath, at that time, all his geometrical theorems some way in him; as also the sleeping musician, all his musical skills and songs; and, therefore, why may it not be possible for the soul to have likewise some actual energy in it, which it is not expressly conscious of?'

John Norris (1632–1704)[10] wrote: 'There are infinitely more ideas impressed on our minds than we can possibly attend to or perceive.' Leibniz (1646–1716), much better known than these writers, spoke of clear ideas as 'islands which arise above the ocean of obscure ones', implying that consciousness accompanies only a small proportion of mental processes, much as is implied in the familiar metaphor of consciousness as the tip of an iceberg (which originated with Fechner, not with Freud).

Thinkers in the eighteenth century were, of course, much influenced by Leibniz. Whyte quotes by way of example the German rationalist C. von Wolff (1679–1752), of whom he says that 'he asserted that less conscious ideas may be the cause of more conscious ones, and he was possibly the first to state explicitly that nonconscious factors must be *inferred* from those of which we are conscious'.[11] In Germany, France and England there were many who continued these lines of philosophical thought, including Rousseau, Hume, Lichtenberg, Kant (who spoke of 'unconscious purpose') and Herder.

Towards the end of the eighteenth century and into the nineteenth century there were three clear streams of concern with the unconscious: the philosophers (e.g. Schelling), the romantic poets (e.g. Goethe and Novalis), and the emerging medical concern with human personality (e.g. Mesmer). It would be out of place to follow their ideas on the unconscious in detail here. The very prominence of their names in the history of thought must suffice to demonstrate Whyte's statement that the unconscious was indeed a topical concern at that time maintained by several increasingly separating intellectual endeavours. Two names, however, must be mentioned here because of their very considerable affinity to Freud's work: Schopenhauer (1788–1860) and C. G. Carus (1789–1869), now a relatively unknown German physician, some of whose works were in Freud's library.

Schopenhauer published his major work, *Die Welt als Wille und Vorstellung*, in 1819, but it achieved its reputation only in the second half of the nineteenth century. As a young man Schopenhauer had paid regular visits to a mental hospital in order to study the interdependence of body and mind. His 'will' is equivalent to the unconscious: man is governed by the irrational forces of the will which consists essentially of two instincts: one for conservation and the second, of much greater power, sexuality. Schopenhauer was influenced by Indian philosophy, and in a cultural pessimism which parallels that of Freud he thought that only the myth of Nirvana promised an end to suffering.

Carus published his major psychological work *Psyche* in 1846. It opens with the following sentence: 'The key to the understanding of the character of the conscious life lies in the region of the unconscious,'[12] and contains a systematic distinction between three layers of the unconscious: the general absolute unconscious which is totally inaccessible to consciousness; the partial absolute unconscious which influences emotions which are consciously experienced, and the secondary unconscious which contains every thought, feeling or perception that was once conscious but had been relegated to the unconscious. Carus was also interested in the interpretation of dreams, but his ideas in that respect were quite different from those of Freud or, for that matter, from those of Schubert (1780–1860) or Scherner, whose book *The Life of the Dream* appeared in 1861, both of whom Freud quotes in the Introduction to *The Interpretation of Dreams*. E. von Hartmann's *The Philosophy the Unconscious* (1869) makes the same distinctions as Carus between three layers of the unconscious and is, according to Whyte, a hotchpotch of ideas from a variety of sources, rather than a systematic treatment. Nevertheless Whyte estimates[13] that about 50,000 Europeans came into contact with its 1,100 pages between 1870–1880, a period in which at least six other books with the term unconscious in the title appeared in Germany, France and England. At the time Freud started his clinical practice every educated person must have become familiar with the idea of the unconscious, if not through the study of these works, then through a process of cultural osmosis which was all the more efficient because the educated élite of Europe was, compared to today, still relatively small.

The gradually emerging conception of European thought

about the unconscious is, of course, closely linked to the next topic, the understanding and treatment of emotional disorders. While it is not immediately obvious how some of the philosophers previously quoted acquired their insights into the unconscious, in Freud's case as much as in that of many of his medical predecessors it stemmed from medical practice. Throughout the ages emotional disorders have both frightened and fascinated those not so afflicted and have been incorporated into general views about the condition of man. While it is of course true that such views differ radically at different epochs and in different places, so that madness was sometimes understood as possession by evil spirits or the devil, sometimes as a holy state, sometimes as punishment for sin, sometimes as a crime and more recently as an illness, under virtually all of these conditions there were some whose special task it was to deal with the afflicted as witchdoctor, shaman, exorcist, inquisitor, custodian or therapist. These practitioners throughout the ages often established a special relationship to the afflicted, a 'transference' if you will, which was sometimes strengthened by a shared belief in the cause of the trouble and a shared purpose in wanting to overcome it. Ellenberger reports a series of apparently well attested and remarkable cures through magic and exorcism which defy any other explanation. It is worth noting that even in our 'scientific' age with all its violent disagreement about the causes of neurotic and psychotic phenomena shared beliefs, shared purpose between therapist and patient, and rapport between them appear to play a major role in achieving cures. It has even been suggested that all new treatments, whether shock, drugs or behaviour therapy, achieve greatest success in the first few years after their introduction, and that when success rates are systematically examined by experts not involved in the invention of a new treatment, they are found to be considerably smaller.

Ellenberger[14] dates the beginning of modern dynamic psychiatry at the period of the 'Enlightenment' and of the extraordinary figure of Mesmer (1734–1815), who combined a belief in his own mysterious healing qualities with a search for 'rational' explanations from the physical sciences of his day, particularly magnetism and electricity. He engaged in a sort of group therapy dealing with twenty persons at a time. He had his successes; and his failures.

Among his students was the Marquis de Puységur (1751–1825) who, Ellenberger says, first used hypnosis—Puységur termed it 'artificial somnabulism'—in the treatment of mental disorders. He treated a twelve-year-old boy by staying with him day and night for six months, thus clearly demonstrating the importance he attached to the relationship between patient and therapist. His major claim to belated recognition, however, appears to lie in his writings on the therapeutic use of hypnosis in which he seems to have anticipated the French school of hypnotists, who played so important a role in the second half of the nineteenth century and in the development of Freud's ideas on the nature and treatment of emotional disorders.

The enormous and world-wide influence of Mesmer and his students until about 1860 can now hardly be imagined. But magnetism and hypnotism fell into disrepute under the influence of positivism and the rationality of the rapidly developing natural sciences, two other profound influences on Freud's thought. For the popular appeal of Mesmerism had rapidly led to the wildest speculations, occultism and spiritism, preoccupation with mediums, ghosts, materialisations and the exploitation of their popularity by charlatans and quacks. However, there was also an effort to study this mixed bag of apparent phenomena scientifically. In 1882 the Society for Psychical Research was founded in England under respectable auspices, and it still functions, actively supported by some members of learned societies.

In any case, during the last quarter of the nineteenth century it took some courage to engage in the discredited practice of hypnosis. Liébault, Bernheim, Charcot and Janet, while disagreeing amongst themselves on many points of method and explanation, had this courage. Freud's familiarity with their work had a profound influence on him which has already been described in a previous chapter, even though his conclusions both on method and theory of neurosis were different from theirs.

Charcot, whom Freud credits with having drawn his attention to the sexual conflict in neurosis by the apparently casual remark 'c'est toujours la chose génitale', denied in his theories that hysteria was a sexual neurosis. But both popular and medical opinion supported the notion that sexual frustration, particularly in women, was responsible for the appearance of neurotic symptoms. An American psychiatrist, Dr. A. J. Ingersoll (1818–1893), saw a causal relationship between hysteria and the voluntary suppression of sexual life, according to Ruitenbeek.[15] Also according to the same author, dynamic interpretations of neurosis as the result of psychological events and the use of dreams for their understanding had been quite frequent in nineteenth-century American psychiatry, as they undoubtedly were in other countries.

Infantile sexuality, too, had been identified by many before Freud. Mothers and nursemaids must have known about it throughout the ages, whatever name they attached to it. Whether they encouraged or condemned it, they could not remain ignorant of the child's interest in his or her sex organs, and of masturbation, let alone of the child's polymorphous pleasure in other skin contacts. The literature on the subject of infantile sexuality seems, however, to have been dominated until well into the nineteenth century by two curious bedfellows: pornographists and moral theologians. To be sure, there were some exceptions, outstanding among them Rousseau's non-pornographic and non-moralising description of that crucial experience of his childhood, the sexual pleasure he derived from being beaten on the buttocks by his aunt.

Ellenberger describes how, in the second half of the nineteenth century, the treatment of sexuality stopped being the exclusive concern of those advocating or condemning sin who had some common ground because they had to describe what they were for or against, and became the subject of systematic study by physicians, psychiatrists and psychologists all over Europe, including Russia. In this transition he assigns pride of place to the Austrian psychiatrist Krafft-Ebing, whose *Psychopathia Sexualis* appeared in 1886, when the author was only twenty-six years old.

Ellenberger and others doubted Freud's claim that his outspokenness on sexuality accounted in part for his early isolation, but it is worth noting that a medical-psychological association threatened to withdraw Krafft-Ebing's honorary membership because he permitted his book to be sold indiscriminately.

Freud himself referred to two physicians who, before him, had clearly noted and described the phenomena of infantile sexuality: a Dr. Lindner who, in 1879, had described thumb-sucking as sexually pleasant, and Dr. Sanford Bell who, by 1902, had collected well over 2,500 observations on infantile sexuality. It is these two sources mentioned by Freud which best exemplify A. N. Whitehead's statement: 'Everything of importance has been said before by somebody who has *not* discovered it.'

This brief discussion of some of Freud's predecessors in three areas of psychoanalytic thought could easily be extended to concepts such as the death instinct, Freud's ideas on memory and thought, repression, the constancy principle or the pleasure principle to name but a few. The main point, however, has been made: there are predecessors to virtually every idea in Freud's work. As Whyte so clearly shows, that is as it must be.

Indeed, the fact that so many independent minds throughout the centuries have made observations similar to those by Freud and proposed ideas and concepts related to those in psychoanalysis makes the appraisal of his work all the more important. It is against this background of so large an heritage in Western thought that the question of Freud's own contribution must be put and answered.

Freud himself said explicitly that he was not interested in claiming priority for psychoanalysis; at various times he suggested various aspects of psychoanalysis as the essence of his contribution; repression, for example, or his method. However engaging the modesty of such claims, they do not sound convincing. Could it be that this conquistador by his own description, restlessly engaged in searching for an understanding of the human mind, felt only intuitively the power of his own contribution but was unable to identify its essence systematically?

It seems to me that the uniqueness of Freud's contribution lies in his construction of an empirically based concept of man which has room for all known psychological phenomena, for mechanism and meaning, for behaviour and action, for feeling, thinking and wishing, for pleasure and reality, for rationality and irrationality, for conscious and unconscious purposes, for body and mind in the unifying experience of being alive, not in a dualistic fashion. I shall return to the implications for psychology of this interpretation of his work in the last chapter. Here it remains to indicate, however briefly, that some elements of this interpretation have indeed already been suggested by others, in particular with regard to Freud's psychological approach to the body-mind problem.

Ricoeur's interpretation has already been indicated; in his view psychoanalysis starts at the point where the somatic finds expression in the experience of desire, but it then turns away from the body which is left as the subject matter for a natural science psychology, a discipline which he regards as quite separate from psychoanalysis. Ferenczi has a related interpretation, even though not the same conclusion, when he says: 'Psychoanalysis, however, dissected human psychic activity, pursued it to the limit where psychic and physical came into contact, down to the instincts . . . To have been the first in the history of science to make this attempt is the achievement of Freud.'[16]

Whyte, even though his book is so profoundly concerned with the problems of dualism, locates Freud's contribution elsewhere: '. . . Freud's supreme achievement was to force the attention of the Western world to the fact that the unconscious mind is of importance in every one of us . . . He was the first systematically to connect the general idea with a wide range of particular distortions of behaviour . . . Freud changed, perhaps irrevocably, man's image of himself. Beside this it is of secondary import that some of his valid ideas were not new, his special conceptions questionable, and his therapeutic methods uncertain.'[17]

Whyte, like a few other commentators on Freud who are sensitive to history and particularly to the history of ideas, sees the time-boundedness of Freud's intellectual contribution. The stumbling block for him, as for Norman O. Brown and for Marcuse, is Freud's pessimism about the human condition, the inseparability of civilisation and repression. In speculating about the possibility of a less tragic conception of man appropriate for a distant future he suggests that Freud's 'Where Id is, there Ego shall be' may then be replaced by 'Where conflict is, there unconscious organic coordination shall be', and he offers his own programmatic formulation for a truly monistic understanding of body and mind when he says: *'Freudian and Non-Freudian psychological conceptions will only be replaced by a more reliable and comprehensive theory of the human mind after exact science has established a valid theory of biological organisation'* (his italics).[18]

Norman O. Brown's powerful book *Life Against Death*, subtitled 'The Psychoanalytic Meaning of History', makes the same point in his very first sentences: 'There is one word which, if we only understand it, is the key to Freud's thought. That word is "repression"'; and he entitles his "way out" in the last chapter "The resurrection of the body", where he says that "the question confronting mankind is the abolition of repression".'[19]

The idea that Freud's central achievement was the understanding of man appropriate to the twentieth century, but that future historical development should and could eliminate repression is also Marcuse's appraisal of Freud's contribution and limitation in *Eros and Civilisation*[20] which appears to have such an extraordinary appeal to a fair proportion of the articulate young of our times. I do not doubt that utopian thought of this kind has its heuristic value. But that it is utopian Marcuse himself recognised in his 'Political Preface 1966' to a new edition of his book, first published in 1955,

which begins thus: 'Eros and Civilisation: the title expressed
an optimistic, euphemistic, even positive thought, namely,
that the achievements of advanced industrial society would
enable man to reverse the direction of progress, to break the
fatal union of productivity and destruction, liberty and
repression . . . This optimism was based on the assumption
that the rationale for the continued acceptance of domina-
tion no longer prevailed, that scarcity and the need for toil
were only "artificially" perpetuated . . . "Polymorphous
sexuality" was the term I used to indicate that the new direction of progress would depend completely on the opportunity
to activate repressed or arrested *organic*, biological needs: to
make the human body an instrument of pleasure rather than
labour. The odds are overwhelmingly on the side of the
powers that be . . . The new boheme, the beatniks and
hipsters, the peace creeps—all of these "decadents" now
have become what decadence probably always was: pure
refuge of defamed humanity', and so on. Notwithstanding
this pessimistic preface, the text remains as it was: a sophisticated discussion of Freud's work denying, however, the
unbreakable link between civilisation and repression which
Freud had stipulated.

However interesting such efforts to eliminate the pessimism
from Freud's conception of man may be in their application
to thoughts about the future of mankind, they have been
presented here for another reason: Whyte's, Brown's and
Marcuse's appreciations of Freud highlight one of his central
achievements: though he tried, and though many psychologists still do, he could not leave the human body to the
attention of physiologists only. He recognised the experience
of one's body as a central psychological event, in the individual's functioning and therefore also in all human creations: in artefacts, in language and in civilisation.

It is, perhaps, appropriate to conclude this selected review
of answers to the questions of what it was that Freud added
to the wealth of related ideas in the work of his predecessors
by a somewhat more sober judgement.

Ellenberger's final appraisal is restrained: 'Whatever the

number of its sources . . . psychoanalytic theory is universally recognised as a powerful and original synthesis . . . Even more than the conceptual framework of psychoanalysis, the psychoanalytic method . . . is Freud's incontestable innovation.'[21] Ellenberger's description of Freud's 'most striking novelty', however, is clearly intended to dampen what he considers unwarranted enthusiasm for Freud's intellectual achievement: 'the founding of a "school" according to a pattern that had no parallel in modern times but is a revival of the old philosophical schools of Greco-Romano antiquity . . . and this is no doubt a noteworthy event in the history of modern culture.'[22]

CHAPTER 9

Freud's Legacy to Psychology

THE history of psychological thought extends backwards to the earliest philosophers whose work has been preserved, and undoubtedly beyond. The history of modern psychology, however, is often—though somewhat arbitrarily—dated from 1879 when Wundt established the first experimental laboratory for psychological research in Leipzig. This was not suggested by Wundt himself, who had a broader view of psychology than was implied in his experimental approach, but by later psychologists who selected the date as a self-conscious declaration of independence from philosophy.

The choice of this particular date and of this particular contribution of Wundt's to psychology entails a deliberate restriction of psychology as a science to those phenomena which lend themselves to investigation by the concepts and methods of the natural sciences.

Wundt, as much as Freud, shared the natural science ethos of the nineteenth century. The triumphant progress of physics, chemistry and physiology, so Wundt argued, was the result of the experimental method. Hence the application of this method to problems of psychology could be expected to produce similar results even though, as he explicitly recognised, one cannot experiment with the 'soul'. Experimental psychology, Wundt thought, was restricted to physiological psychology. In his vocabulary 'soul' meant all higher mental functions; he regarded them, too, as part of the subject of psychology, and in his *Völkerpsychologie* he devoted ten volumes to their exposition. This aspect of his work is now forgotten, and with some justification. Many processes which Wundt assigned to non-experimental psychology—perception and thinking, for example—have since been demonstrated to be amenable to the experimental method. What is worth remembering is that Wundt, the father of experimental psychology, had a conception of the subject which was not tied to *the* scientific method.

Wundt's experimental innovations had an enormous influence on the development of the subject both in the German speaking world, which was then the centre of psychology, as well as in the English speaking world, particularly in the United States, which became the centre after 1933. For many psychologists the methods and concepts of the natural sciences in the nineteenth century became the only article of blind faith in a scientific creed which otherwise extolled the virtue of scepticism. The epistemological underpinning for such a notion of the scope of psychology was provided by the logical positivism of the Vienna circle.

It would be a falsification of the history of psychology in the twentieth century to imply that this mechanistic conception ever achieved the status of a universal paradigm, even though this has been asserted.[1] But there is no doubt that it achieved great power, particularly in the United States under the influence of the behaviourism of J. B. Watson. He took the faith in the method to its logical extreme when he declared that concepts such as perception, memory, consciousness, imagery, feeling or thought were outside the range of a scientific psychology; what remained was stimulus and response.[2]

It is all the more interesting to note that Freud was certainly not opposed to the neo-positivism of the Vienna circle. Not only did he regard himself as a natural scientist; he actively supported positivist efforts. Ellenberger reports that just before the outbreak of the First World War 'a group of scholars founded a *Gesellschaft für positivistische Philosophie* . . . with the aim of arriving at a unified scientific conception of the universe, and thus to solve mankind's problems. Among the members of the society were Ernst Mach, Josef Popper-Lynkeus, Albert Einstein, August Forel, and Sigmund Freud.'[3]

Notwithstanding such demonstrations of faith in psychology as a natural science and in the creed of neo-positivism on the part of Freud, his work cannot be contained within these narrow confines. It is true that he shares with the positivists above all an unwavering determinism with regard to psychological phenomena, a determinism which deals with the experience of free will by regarding it as the result of unconscious motivation. If we knew fully these unconscious determinants of our 'free' choices they would no longer appear 'free'. He never abandoned his hope that physiology would ultimately explain the full complexity of the human mind. The energy concept within the economic metapsychological point of view represents, perhaps, most clearly his natural science stance. Not only does the term stem from physics, but Freud's insistence that psychic energy is measurable in principle emphasises his adherence to an essential aspect of the 'scientific method'.

But when the metapsychological points of view are applied to clinical material with the help of the psychoanalytic method few 'scientific' psychologists would recognise common ground. Freud himself was dismayed early on when he found himself talking a language that sounded more like that of fiction than that of physiology, to which he was used. Like so many psychologists, then and now, he harboured the suspicion that 'good' science was a formal, content-free abstraction from the phenomena under investigation where quantity of energy could stand for the driving force in, say, activating memories or in making love or engaging in stereotyped rituals or responding to praise. This was the spirit of the *Project for a Scientific Psychology*, but it must not be forgotten that Freud refused to publish it during his lifetime. For he had discovered in his clinical work that the physiological reductionism at which the *Project* aimed would force him to abandon the psychological meaning of his observations, and that his main interest in psychology necessitated the creation of a conceptual language which remained applicable to the psychological content of his observations. This he proceeded to do, creating descriptive concepts such as ego, id and super-ego in their relation to each other, describing the oedipal complex, or narcissism, assuming that purposes, conscious and unconscious, could explain behaviour and experiences, and so on.

Implicit in Freud's groping for a conceptual language which was adequate for a description of the functioning of a person in his actual life situation was a language of psychological explanation: while the oedipal complex *describes* a typical life situation, the unconscious is an *explanatory* concept that cannot be directly observed but must be inferred. It is notoriously difficult to distinguish descriptions from explanations, and Freud's descriptive and explanatory concepts shade into each other. But the distinction is not important here. What matters is the creation of a psychological language focusing on the content, concerns and complexities of everyday life without an *a priori* assumption about how to divide human functioning into neat categories which can be studied in isolation from each other.

This is, of course, not meant to underrate the great achievements of academic psychology in doing just this, namely studying memory or perception or learning or attitude change in isolation. Rather the point is that all such studies imply some assumptions about the meaning of such psychological functions within the total organisation of man. To be sure it is not only possible but also necessary to look at, say, cognitive development as Piaget has done without entering simultaneously into the emotional events which may promote or hinder the progression from stage to stage. Nothing in Freud could replace Piaget's achievement in analysing the development of secondary process-type thought. But nothing in Piaget alerts one to the possibility that primary process-type thinking, in which the principle of conservation does not necessarily hold, persists through life. (In Piagetian terminology the principle of conservation refers to the growing child's discovery that one and the same substance can appear in different shapes, whereas a younger child will judge a quantity of water, for example, in a wide dish as 'less' than when the same quantity is poured into a narrower container.) These two psychological languages are complementary rather than contradictory, with Freud's having the wider scope and Piaget's the greater logical coherence.

The first great legacy that Freud left to psychology is thus the creation of a psychological language which has room for all psychological phenomena because it is based on a comprehensive conception and study of man.

But there are, of course, serious problems in Freud's psychological language. Not only is it occasionally inconsistent and often not very clear but Freud, together with many modern psychologists, never fully freed himself from the suspicion that the language of psychology which he had created was not just different from that of physiology, but second best to it. In other words, he would have preferred to be a reductionist, if only his clinical work had permitted it. He tried to translate the language of purpose, intention and conflict in his dynamic point of view into that of cathexis of nerve paths and into forces of different intensity, only to discover that the specific psychological meaning disappeared in the process.

The problem as to whether psychology must, in principle, be reducible to physiology is still with us. It has been treated in a most illuminating way by Margaret Boden in her book *Purposive Explanation in Psychology*,[4] which has, however, not yet penetrated the current level of debate in psychology. Most relevant for the discussion here is a distinction she makes between statements about what man is and statements in conceptual languages in terms of which it makes sense to describe and explain his experiences and behaviour. That man is a physical organism, that mind without body is inconceivable, or in her words 'that purposive phenomena are ... totally dependent on causal (neurophysiological) mechanisms' is uncontested by all psychologists, Freud of course included. But modern science, in contrast to that of antiquity, is no longer concerned with establishing a final world-view about what things essentially are, but rather with discovering ways in terms of which it makes sense to think about phenomena so that their manifestations can be comprehended in an orderly fashion while remaining true to the aspect of the observable world under study. It is possible in psychology to look at man from different points of view, mechanistically or in terms of purposes. As Boden says, however, 'there are certain radical differences between the logic of purposive and mechanistic terms. Consequently the two terminologies are not intertranslatable, and teleological accounts could not be replaced by mechanistic ones without a real loss of explanatory power.'

The realisation that science is in our minds and not 'out there' is both sobering and exhilarating; sobering because it implies that we shall never know the ultimate answers; exhilarating because it promises scientists an indefinite future where there will always be room for inventing new ways of looking at the world which lead to new discoveries.

Karl Popper describes the contrast between ancient and modern ideas of science thus: 'The old scientific ideal of epistémé—of absolute certain, demonstrable knowledge—has proved to be an idol. The demand for scientific objectivity makes it inevitable that every scientific statement must remain *tentative for ever*. It may indeed be corroborated, but every corroboration is relative to other statements which, again, are tentative.'[5]

Freud, as much as many modern psychologists who participate in the debate about the current critical stage of their subject, perpetuates a confusion about these issues. It is as if he had argued: since man *is* a physiological organism, ultimately the most scientific way of *looking* at him must be in terms of neurophysiology. But even though he tried hard it did not work, as has been shown in the discussion of his metapsychological approaches. The analysis of conflict, expressed in the language of forces, lost the meaning of the phenomenon he studied.

Freud's second legacy to psychology stems paradoxically from this very confusion. For the current debate in psychology is carried on between psychologists committed either to a mechanistic view of the subject or to a purposive one. The former claim that they represent the scientific view, but they are accused by the latter of having abandoned psychology's subject matter. Positive and derogatory references to Freud from both sides are frequent in this debate, but his main function in it is that of an irritant, because as a psychologist he spanned both camps. Thus his total work embodies a challenge to create a comprehensive psychology in which meaning and mechanistic causation both have their place; which can be related to each other even though they are expressed in different conceptual languages and not reducible to a single one.

Freud's reductionist belief is in contrast to what he actually did. Had he been consistent he would either have returned to physiology or have excluded from his thought all concern with physiological mechanisms, ignoring the existential indivisibility of body and mind in which he fundamentally believed. There is no sense in speculating on what might have been the outcome of such a consistent choice on his part. But one thing is clear: his significance for modern psychology would have been much reduced. While he might have strengthened one group or the other, he would then have presented a lesser challenge to psychology to conceive of the scientific legitimacy of both.

There are already some indications that there is in the making a new conception of psychology which does not abandon the methods and concepts of the natural sciences but goes beyond them. Cronbach's plea in that direction has already been quoted: he argues for avoiding too narrow a view of psychology as an experimental and highly quantifiable science; for including the humanities in psychology and for understanding rather than prediction from controlled experiments; for a psychology where those who do not confirm a hypothesis are taken as seriously as those who do. Cronbach's general theme has been developed, albeit in a different context, by another leading social psychologist, Donald Campbell.[6] He recommends 'removing any arrogant scientistic certainty that psychology's current beliefs are the final truth . . ., emphasising our need for modesty on topics on which we can do no experiments, broadening our narrowly individualistic focus to include social systems functioning, and expressing a scientifically grounded respect for the wisdom that well-winnowed traditions may contain about how life should be lived'.

Neither of these two psychologists would, of course, wish to deny the great importance of the natural science aspect of psychology. But what they both seem to argue is that psychology as a whole is not just a natural science; that man is to be understood not only mechanistically. Notwithstanding the ambiguities and inconsistencies in Freud's work, so far his is the only system of psychological thought which embodies so broad a view of the subject. Being the only one means being the best only by default. Once the new conception of psychology has fully penetrated the entire field other comprehensive systems of psychology may emerge which are compatible with knowledge acquired since Freud's days; at that time, to venture a prediction, Freud will stop being a figure of controversy and enter an undisputed place in the history of psychology.

But these indications of a broad conception of psychology may only be first swallows. The debate about what is legitimate in psychology as a science continues and is closely interwoven with the debate about the status of psychoanalysis. Whilst there are signs that a broad conception of psychology is emerging which perhaps one day will eliminate Freud's confusion, there are other efforts at coming to terms with him which avoid facing this challenge, so that there is a danger that it may get lost in the turmoil.

Psychoanalysts, some of whom are and some of whom are not knowledgeable in the advances and problems of academic psychology, as well as some university psychologists, contribute their share to this danger. For while these two groups talk, as a rule, about rather different aspects of psychology, there is a formal similarity in the manner in which they deal with the ambiguities, inconsistencies and unresolved problems in Freud's work: for the sake of greater consistency and clarification—both badly needed—they reduce the scope of Freud's conception of psychology. Some neo-Freudian schools eliminate the unconscious and the dominant role of sexuality;

some draw the line against metapsychology,[7] in particular its natural science vocabulary; many 'orthodox' Freudians have never come to terms with the death instinct; some wish to restrict psychoanalysis to the relation between psychoanalyst and analysand. Very few of these debates, however, reach an audience composed of psychologists.

On the academic side the story is much the same: acceptance of isolated aspects of psychoanalysis at the expense of its scope. A study of textbooks in psychology conducted in 1943 revealed a curious pattern in such partial acceptance: 'parts of Freud's theory are being integrated into the general body of knowledge. Acceptance tends to be anonymous, while rejection is personalised.'[8] Other psychologists choose more open ways of confronting Freud. Some, like Gordon Allport, for example, accept the defence mechanisms; some Freud's descriptions and classification of primary thought processes; some the usefulness of the concepts of Ego, Id and Super-ego; some his biological and others his social orientation.

Of course there are also Freudians who take every word he ever wrote as dogma, and university psychologists who condemn it as nonsense. For the purposes of the present argument they can be safely ignored, even though the inadvertent contribution of the latter group to keeping the debate alive should be acknowledged.

It is, of course, conceivable that, from whatever camp it originates, the piecemeal approach to Freud is the only rational way in which psychology at its current fragmented stage can develop. It may be necessary to wait until several of its many branches have reached the end of their particular line and recognise that they need competence in a broader psychological language before the new conception can become acceptable.

Indeed, it would bring psychology to a full stop if all psychologists joined the great debate and abandoned their opportunity to learn from the limitations of their own empirical and theoretical work. But the process of doing research is unfortunately not always conducive to thought; where it is, it occasionally leads to despair and defeatism about psychology, or to a mere switch from one approach to the other, or to the adoption of mysticism and short-lived fads. This is why the debate about the nature of psychology must be kept alive. The discussion of Freud's total work is one way of keeping it so.

Implicit in what has been said is a rejection of Freud's claim that psychoanalysis is a natural science; neither is it a social science, nor a humanistic one, but a combination of the three. This is so not because Freud happened to be gifted in three separate compartments of intellectual pursuit, but because he was a psychologist; and psychology, once the subject of investigation is man rather than single variables, is forced by the results of its own efforts, when taken to their logical conclusion, to use different levels of discourse, even if they are not compatible with each other.

It is also implicit that psychoanalysis is not a theory and, therefore, that efforts to apply validity tests to Freud's total work are beside the point. To be sure, psychoanalysis contains a number of separate theories—on psycho-sexual development, on aggression, on personality, on transference in the clinical situation, etc.—which are open to validity tests, even if we do not yet have the proper techniques for testing the clinical theory. But even if all such tests undermined its validity (and it has already been shown that this is not the case for at least some of the deductions from a Freudian theory) it would leave undamaged this legacy to psychology. Some of Freud's answers may be wrong; his questions are right, because they define the scope of psychology so that what is distinctly human is made the central focus of the discipline. This is what Jerome Bruner must have had in mind when he wrote: 'Freud is the ground from which which theory will grow . . . [he] has provided an image of man that has made him comprehensible without at the same time making him contemptible.'[9]

The question then arises whether a psychology defined by the sum total of Freud's basic questions, not by an arbitrary selection from them, should be regarded as a science at all.

It all depends on what is meant by the term 'science'. Definitions abound but since they are, like all definitions, changeable and ultimately arbitrary, it would be easy enough to adopt a convenient one which includes psychology, or to argue that it does not matter. Much could be said for either argument, but it would miss the point under discussion here. What I am concerned with is to establish an appropriate relationship between psychology and psychoanalysis on the one hand, and the traditionally recognised sciences on the other. This can be done only by adopting the currently entrenched position.

A widely representative definition is offered by Cohen and Nagel[10] in their still influential textbook, which takes scientific method as the defining criterion. On the most general level they describe this method as follows: 'If we look at all the sciences not only as they differ among each other but also as each changes and grows in the course of time, we find that the constant and universal feature of science is its general method, which consists in the persistent search for truth, constantly asking: Is it so? To what extent is it so? Why is it so?—that is, What general conditions or considerations determine it to be so?' Indeed, if these questions represent the essence of the scientific method then psychology and psychoanalysis are scientific enterprises.

The case need hardly be made that academic psychology asks these questions, even though many individual studies are deplorably negligent in dealing with the first of them. It has been reported,[11] for example, that before engaging in their well-known study of imitation Miller and Dollard searched the extensive literature on the topic for descriptions of the phenomenon; they hardly found any, even though there were many categorised references and imaginary examples.

That Freud's thinking followed these questions, on the other hand, needs perhaps another specific illustration. A case in point is his essay entitled 'A Child is Being Beaten'.[12] He begins by establishing the fact that several of his patients reported having indulged in such a phantasy and proceeds to describe it, emphasising common features which consisted of some unidentified adult beating an unidentified child, a scene which gave the originator of the phantasy a sense of pleasure and a tendency to repeat this daydream frequently. Freud did not engage in a statistical study of the frequency of the phenomenon, but contented himself with the assumption that six independent observations of the same highly personal experience in persons who shared only the fact that they suffered from neurotic symptoms and were in analysis justified a search for a common cause of this phantasy. In other words, he asked what conditions or considerations determined the phenomenon. He answered it in terms of his psycho-sexual theory.

But apparently Cohen and Nagel's very general formulation of the essence of scientific method, and Freud's adherence to it to the extent that has been illustrated, do not meet the critical point which is often made that Freud abandoned science when he left physiological research: this point, of course, concerns the psychoanalytic method proper. This is *de facto* a method outside the well established canon of scientific procedure in both its aspects: as a method for data collection and as a method for testing the validity of interpretations. Ricoeur and Habermas argue that because of the peculiarities of this method, which is central to psychoanalysis, it should not be classed with other sciences but be regarded perhaps as a *Geisteswissenschaft*, but more appropriately as part of philosophy, as hermeneutics would be regarded in the English-speaking world. It is perhaps well to add that neither Ricoeur nor Habermas see in their understanding of psychoanalysis as hermeneutics a 'degradation' of its intellectual status. If anything the contrary is true. Their arguments are indeed powerful and persuasive. I fear, however, that if this were to be accepted now as a final verdict, psychology and psychoanalysis would most likely arrive at an irrevocable split. This would make it less likely that psychologists will examine their own critical problems in the light of lessons to be learned from psychoanalysis or that psychoanalysts will learn from psychology how to improve on Freud's psychology which, after all, went beyond hermeneutics. It is impossible to predict where such mutual learning will leave psychology in the future, unified or divided in the traditional way or according to new lines, not yet firmly drawn. But it is reasonable to expect that it will be in a clearer position than it is now. If the psychoanalytic method were indefensible one would, of course, have to settle for the split; but then it should be classed with crystal gazing or astrology (the latter is now being treated with probability statistics in a most respectable fashion) rather than with hermeneutics or a combination of sciences.

The dilemma really comes down to this: do available methods, sanctioned by their similarity to natural science procedures, define the problems which are legitimate research topics in psychology, or do legitimate problems require the invention of new methods appropriate to them? It is well to remember that Aristotle already resolved this dilemma when he wrote in the *Nichomachean Ethics* that the educated mind will insist on precision in so far as the nature of the subject permits.

Freud's method was new in his time; it evolved out of his disenchantment with the techniques available in his day for the cure of neurosis. It developed into a research method because Freud remained true to the scientific principle of observing in minute detail everything relevant to his chosen question: why did his patients suffer? This led him inevitably to the bigger problem: how can one understand the structure and functioning of the mind? He designed a method for the fullest possible exploration of the content of a person's mind without arbitrary exclusion. Of course he had his own pre-conceived ideas; but then no observation is possible without a point of view, as Darwin already knew. When he had enough material forming tentative support for one of his guiding notions he suggested it to the patient, and took certain indicators of the impact of such an interpretation as a verification or falsification of his guesses, rather than relying on a 'yes' or 'no' answer.

What makes this method different from other psychological

research? Perhaps the strongest difference lies in the fact that it is a joint enterprise between two persons, each of whom is performing a special role, but both required to be intellectually active and both agreed on the common goal of understanding the patient's experiences. This type of collaborative effort between the analyst and the person under study is absent from 'objective' psychology.

Leaving aside the therapeutic value of this method, it can and has been criticised. For the emerging data are, of course, influenced by the interaction between the participants and the unique situation in which they find themselves, particularly through the establishment of transference and countertransference. This is indisputable, though not unacceptable. For all other methods available to psychology have their specific shortcomings too. The psychological experiment is at least as unique a situation as the analytic couch, since it allocates to its subjects a totally passive and often deliberately mystifying role without establishing a common purpose. It could be argued that it is an even stronger modification of the manner in which people normally function than the analytic situation. What is equally important is that recent experiments on experiments have demonstrated that there is a real danger that the expectations of the experimenter may influence the results he obtains; there is even reason to believe that this danger plagues the natural sciences too. In addition, experiments involve a very short-lived contact between experimenter and subject. For Freud's research purpose observation and interaction over hundreds of hours were required, a fact which implies that he had at his disposal more samples of the functioning mind than an experimenter, seeing his patient before transference had developed, during positive and negative transference periods and, one hopes, at a final stage when transference was resolved.

This is not to say that Freud's great technique for an exploration of the mind approached Brunswick's request for systematic sampling of situations,[13] only that it is somewhat closer to it than psychological experiments normally are. Yet no one would argue that experiments should be excluded from the repertoire of psychological methods, for they present the strictest test of assumptions that has yet been devised. With all their pitfalls, for this purpose no better technique exists, as long as the phenomena under investigation are not simplified out of existence by the experimental manipulation. For Freud's purpose, the mapping of the mind, they are nonetheless as unsuitable as they would have been for Darwin's naturalistic observations. The narrow identification of science with the experimental method was singled out by Koch as the major factor which prevented psychology from remaining true to its subject matter. He wrote: 'From the earliest days of the experimental pioneers, the stipulation that psychology be adequate to *science* outweighed the commitment that it be adequate to man . . .'[14]

Of course the psychoanalytic method can be and has been mishandled, as has every other technique. There are many examples available in the literature to demonstrate this. Freud himself, as has been described in an early chapter, was certainly not immune to making avoidable mistakes. In his early days as a psychoanalyst he seems to have imposed his theory more vigorously on his patients than his belief in the importance of observation warranted. But he learned to conform to his scientific credo, and he said again and again that he expected his theoretical formulations to be changed or discarded; what must remain, he thought, were the observations from which they were inferred. The sexual element in the symptoms of neurosis was not a theoretical stipulation but an inference from observing his patients, listening for many hours to their conscious difficulties with their sexual partners or with the absence of such partners, their fears and hopes, dreams and desires. The understanding of the transference situation, anticipating as it does his later formulation of the repetition compulsion, was possible only through painstaking continuous observation of details which he continuously confronted with the question: why? In this context it is of interest to note that when Freud finally formulated his concept of repetition compulsion he linked it to an observation of his grandson, who invented a repetitive game in an effort

—so Freud interpreted it—to come to terms with the absence of his mother. This game is the 'Fort-da' (gone-here) episode described in *Beyond the Pleasure Principle*, of which Lacan[15] makes so much in his discussion of Freud.

The emphasis on observation and the involvement with the process of data collection is another aspect of Freud's legacy to psychology. Admittedly, this is only one stage of the research process, but one whose importance is all too often underrated. Many survey-researchers have never conducted a single interview themselves; indeed, it is an inevitable shortcoming of this valuable technique that involvement in the collection of the raw data must be the task of persons less well trained than the investigator in charge of the survey. Experimental psychologists often delegate the opportunity to observe how rats or people behave in the research situation to assistants, if not to a computer programmed to record preselected categories of response. Once again, this is not to argue that such division of labour in research is illegitimate in itself. It has its uses, but only when somebody has first undertaken the trouble of immersing himself in the observation of the phenomenon under study. It is certainly an incongruous situation in social psychology, for example, that there is a voluminous research literature on theories and experiments concerning attitude change, but not a single descriptive account of how such changes actually occur outside the laboratory situation.[16]

Fortunately not all psychologists eschew observation. Participant observation, with its own problem of observer and observed influencing the data and each other in a peculiar transference problem, has long been recognised as an important technique, which is even amenable to some quantification.[17] The Russian psychologist Luria[18] has, within the last few years, enriched the psychological literature immensely by reporting his detailed observations of two persons, collected over a period of some twenty years. One of them exhibited an extraordinary condition of memory: he could not forget. The other concerns a young soldier who received a bullet in his brain; Luria helped him to relearn to understand, speak, read and even write. More recently, the observational methods of ethology have been adapted for psychological research purposes. It is perhaps no accident that the foremost representative of this new development, John Bowlby,[19] is also a trained psychoanalyst. And yet this method too has, in its current state of development, its peculiar shortcoming in addition to its great promise; for by definition it excludes the confrontation between the private world of the observed and the perspective of the observer, which is built into the psychoanalytic method.

The term 'private world' needs explication and qualification, for it implies another bone of contention about the status of psychoanalysis. Private worlds, it is argued, are in principle inaccessible to scientific methods. This is so, if by 'private' we understand assumed internal events which defy expression in gestures or language. But this is not what is meant by the privacy of the psychoanalytic situation which depends entirely on what is communicable. Private here is understood as in contrast to what one would be inclined to communicate publicly. But it must be communicated and, therefore, far from being a solipsism à deux, it is in principle observable by independent observers. Indeed, video-taped records of analytic sessions are already available in the United States and are being used for the training of psychoanalysts; they still await exploitation for research purposes.

All this supports the notion that there is nothing in the psychoanalytic method which disqualifies psychoanalysis from scientific status. Like every other method it has its problems and shortcomings, and more than others it is time-consuming, expensive, difficult to learn and open to misuse. But for the purposes for which Freud designed it there exists no substitute so far.

Once the inherent limitations of a particular method are recognised, the remedy lies at hand: other methods whose shortcomings are elsewhere are called for to complement inferences. What about the psychoanalytic method in this respect? Freud, as has been shown, was not very receptive to

the idea that experimental demonstrations of the phenomenon of repression added anything to his knowledge of it.
He had a point, because his method permitted him to discover the meaningful content of what was repressed and its
eruption into unexpected areas of consciousness, while the
experimental demonstration could not deal with the ramifi-
cations of the phenomenon.[20] But his judgement in this case
embodies a mistake in his pursuit of his fundamental aim of
contributing to a general psychology. He could not really
have believed that this was a one-man task; science, he knew
as well as anybody, is above all a collective exercise to which
methodologically and ideologically independent approaches
to one and the same phenomenon are crucial.

However, while he did write the now well known condescending letter to the experimental psychologist Rosenzweig which has already been quoted, he himself engaged in
other forms of testing his inferences. I have suggested before
that Freud's excursions into other fields such as anthropology,
history, art and literature served exactly this purpose. There
is no need to repeat the argument here. What should be added
is another aspect of Freud's legacy to psychology: a demonstration of how to be interdisciplinary.

Interdisciplinary research is rightly on the agenda of many
modern psychologists, for the social problems which they are
increasingly called upon to tackle—poverty, inflation,
violence, delinquency, racial conflict, to name but a few—
have as a rule been approached before by non-psychological
disciplines, all of which have some contribution to make to
an understanding of these problems. The logic of interdisciplinary research, however, has not yet been spelled out.
It is sometimes interpreted as the collection under one cover
of studies of a phenomenon in the separate languages of the
various disciplines based on their various preferred forms of
data collection, in the hope that a reader will integrate in his
mind what research could not combine. Other interdisciplinary efforts do not rely on such pious hopes, but attempt
a combination of the various languages in the human sciences
in the conduct of research. This is feasible when not more

than two disciplines are involved, but at a price which is most often the abandonment of hard-won theoretical formulations in each single discipline. The most obvious example is the interdisciplinary combination of psychology and sociology in that peculiar hybrid—social-psychology—which, though it produces so many interesting and important studies, has not got a theory to its name which is interdisciplinary. The theoretical formulations within social-psychology are either clearly psychological or clearly sociological.

I do not know whether truly interdisciplinary theories are possible; they may not even be necessary for some empirical problems where ad-hoc generalisations can serve a useful function. However this may be, the point here is to draw attention to Freud's interpretation of psychology's relation to other fields which, even though it does not fulfil the noble aims of the positivist society of which he was a member, promises at least to advance psychology. He was inter-disciplinary not by losing his identity as a psychologist, let alone by abandoning any of his theoretical formulations, but by looking at the phenomena and their regularities which form the data for other disciplines rather than at their con-ceptual formulations, and interpreting them in psychological terms. Nothing in his interpretation of the dreams in Jensen's *Gradiva*, a novel regarded by experts as rather second-rate, was presented as literary criticism; nothing in *Totem and Taboo* qualifies as a contribution to anthropology; nothing in *Moses and Monotheism* resembles historical research; no-thing in *Civilization and Its Discontents* is a substitute for socio-logical, economic or political analysis. But each of these works served Freud as a testing ground for the validity of his psychological ideas.

Interdisciplinary work so interpreted shows a way in which Cronbach's and Campbell's plea for broadening psychology by the inclusion of history, anthropology and the humanities could be implemented without destroying the identity of psychology as a subject. This approach will not emerge with a universal scientific language. All it can achieve is to enlarge the testing ground for psychology and, in doing so, perhaps also illuminate the tacit assumptions about psychological processes which other disciplines dealing with man in society inevitably have to make.

Needless to say there are dangers and difficulties in this approach too, exemplified by Freud himself. For he used his excursions into other fields not to see whether he was right, but to allay his doubts, to *prove* that he was right. In fairness it should be emphasised that this is after all what all scientists capable of creative ideas attempt to do.

Falsification is always left to others. Psychologists so far have not tried to compete with Freud's interdisciplinary efforts in any systematic fashion; they have not yet faced the problem of external validity for their entire approach to the study of man. Once they accept this particular challenge of Freud's work they will be in a better position to argue for or against him.

It need hardly be said that Freud's word is not the last word in psychology; in the development of disciplined thought there cannot be a last word. His legacy consists of a set of challenges, not of a set of final answers. Those psychologists who have come to terms with the body of his work can hope to transcend him; those who have not continue to be irritated by the evidence of his persistent impact on the subject. For the best of them are aware that much of the contemporary research literature in the technical psychological journals consists of 'elegant trivialities', to use Gordon Allport's critical phrase; that is, of sophisticated quantitative methods applied to insignificant questions. But they also sense that Freud was never trivial; his questions remain significant.

It is true, however, that in testing his psychological ideas by applying them to historical, cultural and philosophical issues, Freud imposed on psychoanalysis the world-view of his old age. Even though he had warned psychoanalysts against forcing their own philosophy of life on their patients, outside the consulting room he himself disregarded such restrictions. Like the scientists of antiquity and in contrast to modern scientists he searched for final answers about the essence of the human conditions and he emerged with a fundamentally tragic conception of man: the inescapable existential unity of body and mind implies inescapable suffering; man's greatest achievements are possible only at the expense of forgoing the gratification of bodily demands; repression of sexuality is the price to be paid for civilisation; only barbarians can be healthy; the aim of all life is death.

It is not always easy to disentangle in Freud's writings his own personal philosophy from his contribution to psychology. There can be no doubt that there is more in Freud, as in all of us, than befits a science of psychology. The peculiar dilemmas of all psychology, not just of psychoanalysis, arise in large measure from the relevance of all psychological thought to each person's life experience. Psychology is reflexive and its practitioners are driven by their own work to ask questions which no science can answer. There are public and private ways of living with such questions. Freud made his public and in doing so rejected religion as an illusion, even though he realised, of course, that it had for millions the power to answer the unanswerable.

Some of the most outstanding commentators have taken issue with the profound pessimism of Freud's old age. It has been mentioned before that Whyte put his faith in a biological science which would one day eliminate inner conflict; Norman Brown dreams of an age of innocence without repression; Marcuse hopes that social revolution will mitigate, if not eliminate, tragedy from the human condition. The most recent comment on Freud's pessimism as it emerges in his studies of history and civilisation is contained in a brilliant book by Ernest Becker, *The Denial of Death*;[21] he rightly criticises such dreams as naive and finds his own solution in mystical religious feelings which transcend the conditions of the body.

Psychoanalysts, psychologists and even natural scientists arrive inevitably face to face with the great riddles which, as scientists, they lack the competence to solve. Within a much more modest frame of mind, a psychologist will not mistake Freud's world-view for part of his science. He may compare

Freud's triumphant suggestion as a young man that a plaque would one day be fixed to his house with the inscription: 'Here the secret of the Unconscious was revealed to Sigmund Freud', with the words of his old age that 'the aim of all life is death'; and wonder.

Notes

INTRODUCTION

(1) *The Index to Psychoanalytic Writings*, compiled and edited by Alexander Grinstein (New York, International Universities Press, 1975).

(2) Philip Rieff, *Freud: the Mind of the Moralist* (London, Gollancz, 1959), p. x.

(3) L. Trilling, *Freud and the Crisis of our Culture* (New York, Beacon Press, 1955).

CHAPTER 1

(1) Ernest Jones, *Sigmund Freud, Life and Work*, Vols 1, 2 and 3 (London, The Hogarth Press; New York, Basic Books, 1953–1957).

(2) H. F. Ellenberger, *The Discovery of the Unconscious* (New York, Basic Books; London, Allen Lane The Penguin Press, 1970). Even so remarkable a scholar is not free from inconsistencies. He speaks of three marriages on p. 425; on p. 468, however, Freud's mother is identified as Jacob's second wife.

(3) *The Interpretation of Dreams* (1900), *Standard Edition*, Vol. 4.

(4) *An Autobiographical Study* (1925), *Standard Edition*, Vol. 20.

(5) Joseph and Renée Gicklhorn, *Sigmund Freud's akademische Laufbahn im Lichte der Dokumente* (Vienna, 1960).

(6) K. R. Eissler, *Sigmund Freud und die Wiener Universität* (Bern, 1966).

(7) Friedrich Heer, 'Freud, the Viennese Jew', in Jonathan Miller (ed), *Freud, the Man, his World, his Influence* (London, Weidenfeld and Nicolson, 1972).

(8) A. Janick and S. Toulmin, *Wittgenstein's Vienna* (London, Weidenfeld and Nicolson, 1973).

(9) *The Origins of Psycho-Analysis* (London, The Hogarth Press; New York, Basic Books, 1954).

(10) Carl E. Schorske, 'Politics and Patricide in Freud's *Interpretation of Dreams*', *Amer. Hist. Review* (1973), Vol. 78, pp. 328–47.

(11) Ernest Jones, *op. cit.*, Vol. 1, pp. 360–61.

(12) 'The Psychogenesis of a Case of Homosexuality in a Woman' (1920), *Standard Edition*, Vol. 18.

(13) 'On Transformations of Instinct as Exemplified in Anal Erotism' (1917), *Standard Edition*, Vol. 17.

(14) 'On Psychotherapy' (1905), *Standard Edition*, Vol. 7, p. 259. See also Vol. 16, *Introductory Lectures*, 'Analytic Therapy'.

(15) 'Lines of Advance in Psychoanalytic Therapy' (1919), *Standard Edition*, Vol. 17, p. 167.

(16) *An Outline of Psycho-Analysis* (1938), *Standard Edition*, Vol. 23, p. 182.

(17) 'Analysis Terminable and Interminable' (1937), *Standard Edition*, Vol. 23.

(18) *Psychoanalysis and Faith: the Letters of Sigmund Freud and Oskar Pfister* (London, The Hogarth Press; New York, Basic Books, 1963).

(19) Otto Rank, *The Trauma of Birth* (1924) (London, Kegan Paul, 1929).

(20) 'Fixation to Traumas—The Unconscious' (1917), *Standard Edition*, Vol. 16.

(21) H. J. Eysenck, 'The Effects of Psychotherapy: An Evaluation', *J. Consult. Psych.* (1952), **16**, 319–24.

(22) A. E. Bergin and Sol. L. Garfield (eds), *Handbook of Psychotherapy and Behaviour Change: An Empirical Analysis* (New York, Wiley, 1971).

(23) Paul Kline in his meticulous *Fact and Fantasy in Freudian Theory* (London, Methuen, 1972), has examined the uproar which followed Eysenck's article in the research literature, quoting Eysenck as later admitting that he overstated his case so as to stimulate research! Kline, on all the evidence at his disposal, comes to the conclusion that the effect of psychoanalysis as a therapy is not yet convincingly established.

(24) O. F. Kernberg, E. D. Burstein, L. Coyne, A. Applebaum, L. Horwitz and H. Voth, *Psychotherapy and Psychoanalysis: Final Report of the Menninger Foundation's Psychotherapy Research Project* (Topeka, Kansas, The Menninger Foundation, 1972), pp. x; 275.

(25) These are, of course, private matters which can be made public only by the psychologists themselves. Some of them have done so: Neal Miller, Hilgard, Murphy, Boring, Piaget, Philip Rieff, Else Frenkel-Brunswick, M. Brewster Smith, but also J. B. Watson (see his somewhat oblique reference in his autobiography in Carl Murchison, et al., eds, *A History of Psychology in Autobiography* (Worcester, Mass., 1930–65) III, 274), Gardner Lindzey, George S. Klein, Robert Holt, etc. Unavoidably I have also to add M. Jahoda. Also the sociologist Talcott Parsons and undoubtedly many others.

(26) Preface to Reik's *Ritual* (1919), *Standard Edition*, Vol. 17, p. 259.

(27) *The Future of an Illusion* (1927), *Standard Edition*, Vol. 21, p. 36.

(28) David Bakan, *Sigmund Freud and the Jewish Mystical Tradition* (Princeton, Van Nostrand, 1958).

(29) Frank Cioffi, 'Was Freud a Liar?', *The Listener* (7 Feb., 1974), **91**. See also Robert Borger and Frank Cioffi, eds, *Explanations in the Behavioural Sciences* (Cambridge University Press, 1970); Frank Cioffi, 'Freud and the Idea of a Pseudo-Science', p. 471ff.

(30) Cioffi's 'amnesia' theory overlooks the fact that Freud was, soon

after the publication of the seduction theory, fully aware of his own intellectual doubts about it. On 31 May, 1897 he wrote to Fliess to that effect. In his letter he interprets one of his own dreams as fulfilling 'my wish to pin down a father as the originator of neurosis and put an end to my persistent doubts'. In *The Origins of Psychoanalysis*, *op. cit.*, p. 206.

(31) R. Borger and F. Cioffi, *op. cit.*

(32) P. Kline, *op. cit.* This contains a discussion of about 500 experimental tests of Freudian hypotheses, and it is not comprehensive. 'The Resistances to Psychoanalysis' (1925), *Standard Edition*, Vol. 19.

(33) *An Autobiographical Study* (1925), *Standard Edition*, Vol. 20.

(34) *Studies on Hysteria* (1893–5), *Standard Edition*, Vol. 2.

(35) *Jokes and their Relation to the Unconscious* (1905), *Standard Edition*, Vol. 8.

(36) *The Psychopathology of Everyday Life* (1901), *Standard Edition*, Vol. 6.

(37) 'A Special Type of Choice of Object Made by Men' (1910), *Standard Edition*, Vol. 11, p. 165.

(38) P. B. Medawar, 'Victims of Psychiatry', *The New York Review of Books*, 23 Jan., 1975.

(39) K. Popper, 'Philosophy of science: a personal report', *Brit. Philos. in Mid-Century, 1957*. C. A. Mace (ed), London. 'And as for Freud's epic of the Ego, the Superego, and the Id, no substantially stronger claim to scientific status can be made for it than for Homer's collected stories from Olympus. These theories describe some facts, but in the manner of myths they contain most interesting psychological suggestions, but not in a testable form.'

(40) S. Hook (ed), *Psychoanalysis, Scientific Method and Philosophy* (New York U.P., 1959).

(41) Barbara Wootton, *Testament for Social Science* (London, Allen & Unwin, 1950), p. 176.

(42) 'The Resistances to Psycho-Analysis' (1925), *Standard Edition*, Vol. 19, p. 217.

(43) *An Outline of Psycho-Analysis* (1938), *Standard Edition*, Vol. 23, p. 158.

(44) A. C. McIntyre, *The Unconscious, a Conceptual Study* (London, Routledge & Kegan Paul, 1958), p. 48.

(45) J. Habermas, *Knowledge and Human Interest* (New York, Beacon Press, 1971).

(46) E. Jones, *op. cit.*, Vol. 1, Appendix.

(47) H. Orlansky, 'Infant Care and Personality', *Psychol. Bulletin* (1949), **46**.

(48) R. R. Sears, *Survey of Objective Studies of Psychoanalytic Concepts* (New York, Social Science Research Council, 1947).

(49) P. Kline, *op. cit.*

CHAPTER 2

(1) *An Autobiographical Study* (1925), *Standard Edition*, Vol. 20.

(2) *Studies on Hysteria* (1893–5), *Standard Edition*, Vol. 2; 'A Case of Successful Treatment by Hypnotism' (1892–3), *Standard Edition*, Vol. 1.

(3) 'From the History of an Infantile Neurosis' (1918), *Standard Edition*, Vol. 17. See also Muriel Gardiner, ed, *The Wolf-Man and Sigmund Freud* (London, The Hogarth Press; New York, Basic Books, 1972), which contains not only Freud's case study and the later treatment of the patient by Ruth Mack-Brunswick, but also the patient's autobiographical account, written at the age of 83 years.

(4) See, e.g., the Wolf-Man's report on his hypnotic session in Russia. A comprehensive and truly fascinating account of the history of hypnotism can be found in Ellenberger, *op. cit.*

(5) Freud's relation with Breuer has become another biographical controversy. See Jones and Ellenberger, *op. cit.*

(6) *Project for a Scientific Psychology* (1895), *Standard Edition*, Vol. 1.

(7) *Ibid.*, p. 295.

(8) *The Origins of Psycho-Analysis*, *op. cit.*, p. 26.

(9) K. H. Pribram, 'The Neuropsychology of Sigmund Freud', in A. J. Bachrach, ed, *Experimental Foundations of Clinical Psychology* (New York, Basic Books, 1962).

(10) This procedure finds an analogue in M. Brewster Smith, Jerome S. Bruner and Robert W. White, *Opinions and Personality* (New York, Wiley, 1956), where the authors report on the effect of a stress interview.

(11) See, e.g., T. R. Miles, *Eliminating the Unconscious: A Behaviourist View of Psychoanalysis* (Pergamon, 1966), in which he gives many examples of reification in Freud's work, and suggests that if we had a language of verbs rather than nouns (other than for objects) psychoanalysis would have been easier to accept.

(12) *An Outline of Psychoanalysis* (1938), *Standard Edition*, Vol. 23.

(13) 'The Unconscious' (1915), *Standard Edition*, Vol. 14.

(14) 'Lecture XXVIII: Analytic Therapy' (1917), *Standard Edition*, Vol. 16.

(15) Margaret Brenman and Merton M. Gill, *Hypnotherapy* (New York, International Universities Press, 1971); first published in 1944 by the Josiah Macy, Jr., Foundation in its *Review Series*.

(16) What exactly produced that break is controversial. Jones, Ellenberger, Kris and others have given varying accounts of the episode. Kris' account in the introduction to the Freud-Fliess correspondence (*The Origins of Psycho-Analysis*, *op. cit.*) is not entirely borne out by the letters themselves which describe on several occasions Breuer's support,

doubt, renewed public support and private doubt about Freud's ideas on sexuality.

(17) Brenman and Gill, *op. cit.*, seem to have found a way of making this possible, however.

(18) *Standard Edition*, Vol. 3, pp. 209–10.

(19) *Standard Edition*, Vol. 3.

(20) See Chapter 2, note 25.

(21) *Inhibitions, Symptoms and Anxiety* (1926), *Standard Edition*, Vol. 20, p. 149.

(22) Borger and Cioffi, *op. cit.*, p. 509.

(23) James D. Watson, *The Double Helix* (New York, Atheneum, 1968).

(24) *Standard Edition*, Vol. 2, pp. 275–6.

(25) 'The Unconscious' (1915), Appendix C, *Standard Edition*, Vol. 14.

(26) *On Aphasia* (1891).

(27) See Paul Roazen, *Brother Animal* (New York, Knopf, 1969; London, Allen Lane), and his book *Freud and his Followers* (New York, Knopf, 1975; London, Allen Lane, 1976). Roazen started in 1964 to interview those still alive who had known Freud personally. He managed to reach over seventy persons, twenty-five of whom had been Freud's psychoanalytic patients. This historically most interesting material adds less than one might have expected to our knowledge of the development of the psychoanalytic method. Roazen's earlier book has given rise to a particularly bitter controversy over Freud's relation to Victor Tausk, a psychoanalyst in the making, who committed suicide.

(28) *An Autobiographical Study* (1925), *Standard Edition*, Vol. 20.

(29) Reuben Fine, *Freud: A Critical Re-evaluation of his Theories* (London, Allen & Unwin, 1962), p. 37.

(30) Roazen, *Brother Animal*, *op. cit.*, however, reports that Freud, contrary to these injunctions, analysed his daughter Anna.

(31) Freud has not provided, in one place, a full and comprehensive description of the features of psychoanalytic therapy. Discussions of some length can be found in the *Introductory Lectures* (*Standard Edition*, Vols 15 and 16), *An Autobiographical Study* (*Standard Edition*, Vol. 20), *The Question of Lay Analysis* (*Standard Edition*, Vol. 20), in 'Analysis Terminable and Interminable' (*Standard Edition*, Vol. 23), and in his papers on technique.

(32) See particularly Chapter VII in *The Interpretation of Dreams*.

(33) See, for example, N. S. Sutherland, *Breakdown* (London, Weidenfeld and Nicolson, 1976), who describes his unhappy experience with psychoanalytic therapy.

(34) Philip Rieff, *Freud: the Mind of the Moralist* (London, Gollancz, 1959), p. 332.

(35) Karl Bühler, *Die Krise der Psychologie* (1929).

(36) In addition to previous references, the intensive public debate on F. Skinner's *Beyond Freedom and Dignity* (London, Jonathan Cape, 1972), is the best example of the difficulty of dealing with this particular frustration in academic psychology.

(37) Michel Foucault, *The Order of Things: An Archeology of the Human Sciences* (London, Tavistock, 1970) p. xxiii.

(38) An American psychologist, S. Rosenzweig, had sent Freud his report on some experimental demonstration of repression in the early thirties. Freud replied:

'My dear Sir,

I have examined your experimental studies for the verification of the psychoanalytic assertions with interest. I cannot put much value on these confirmations because the wealth of reliable observations on which these assertions rest make them independent of experimental verification. Still, it can do no harm.

Sincerely yours,
Freud.'

Quoted from D. Shakov and D. Rapaport, *The Influence of Freud on American Psychology* (Cleveland, World Pub., 1968), p. 129.

(39) G. S. Klein, 'Consciousness in Psychoanalytic Theory: Some Implications for Current Research in Perception', *J. American Psychoanal. Assn.* (1959), **1**, 5–34.

CHAPTER 3

(1) Letter dated 25 May, 1895, *The Origins of Psycho-Analysis*, pp. 119–20.

(2) 'The Goethe Prize' (1930), *Standard Edition*, Vol. 21, p. 207.

(3) Paul Roazen, *Sigmund Freud* (New York, Prentice Hall, 1973), p. 4.

(4) *The Interpretation of Dreams* (1900), *op. cit.*

(5) Not surprisingly, Freud scholars have seized the opportunity inherent in Freud's analysis of his own dreams to make inferences about the man. See, for example, Didier Anzieu in his *L'Auto-analyse de Freud* (Paris, 1959), who established the chronology of these dreams; or Grinstein, *On Sigmund Freud's Dreams* (Detroit, 1968). One of the most interesting interpretations is contained in Carl E. Schorske, 'Politics and Patricide in Freud's Interpretations of Dreams', *The American Historical Review, op. cit.*, who argues that 'Freud was engaged in a "life-long struggle" with Austrian socio-political reality: as a scientist and Jew, as citizen and son.' He 'overcame it by devising an epoch-making interpretation of human experience in which politics could be reduced to an epiphenomenal manifestation of psychic forces'.

(6) Dreams are discussed in virtually all of Freud's expository writings and in his case studies. Specific publications are: 'The Handling of Dream-Interpretation in Psychoanalysis' (1911), *Standard Edition*, Vol. 12; 'Dreams' (1916), *Standard Edition*, Vol. 15; 'A Metapsychological Supplement to the Theory of Dreams' (1915), *Standard Edition*, Vol. 14; 'Remarks on the Theory and Practice of Dream Interpretation' (1922), *Standard Edition*, Vol. 19; 'Revision of the Theory of Dreams' (1932), *Standard Edition*, Vol. 22.

(7) Talcott Parsons, '*The Interpretation of Dreams* by Sigmund Freud', *Daedalus* (Winter 1974), pp. 91–6, Twentieth Century Classics Revisited.

(8) This chapter should be read by the many psychologists who assert that Freud ignored the work of others. W. S. Taylor, e.g. in 'Psycho-analysis Revised or Psychodynamics Developed?', *American Psychologist* (November 1962), accused Freud of having read little psychology and overlooking Herbart. Herbart, however, is quoted by Freud in this chapter. Other psychologists quoted in the book are: Busemann, Claparède, Fechner, Galton, Garnier, Jodl, Lipps, Maudsley, Meynert, Myers, Nelson, Pötzl, Morton Prince, Roffenstein, Scherner, Schleiermacher, Schubert, Stricker, Stumpf, Wundt (excluding many relevant philosophers and all psychoanalytic work).

(9) Seymour M. Berger and William W. Lambert, 'Stimulus-Response Theory in Contemporary Social Psychology', p. 86, in Gardner Lindzey and Elliot Aronson (eds), *The Handbook of Social Psychology*, Vol. 1, Second edition (Addison-Wesley, 1968).

(10) Frank Cioffi, 'Wittgenstein's Freud', p. 184 in Peter Winch (ed) *Studies in the Philosophy of Wittgenstein* (London, Routledge & Kegan Paul, 1969).

(11) Hutchins Hapgood, *A Victorian in the Modern World* (New York, 1939), quoted in David Shakov and David Rapaport, *The Influence of Freud on American Psychology*, Psychological Issues 4, No. 1, Monograph 13, 1964, p. 41.

(12) It is of some interest that in 1764 Kant expressed a similar view in an Essay on the Diseases of the Mind: 'We need not assume that our soul, while we are awake, is governed by different laws from those we are subject to while we are asleep.' In: I. Kant, *Dreams of a Spirit Seer and Other Early Essays* (New York, Vantage Press, 1969).

(13) *The Interpretation of Dreams* (1900), *Standard Edition*, Vol. 5, p. 511.

(14) David Rapaport, 'The Conceptual Model of Psychoanalysis', in D. Krech and G. S. Klein (eds), *Theoretical Models and Personality Theory* (New York, Duke University Press, 1952).

(15) *Ibid.*

(16) *Standard Edition*, Vol. 5, p. 598.

(17) *Standard Edition*, Vol. 4, p. 151.

(18) 'The Handling of Dream-Interpretation in Psychoanalysis' (1911), *Standard Edition*. Vol. 12.

(19) D. Broadbent, *Perception and Communication* (New York, Pergamon Press, 1958).

(20) *Standard Edition*, Vol. 4, p. 299.

(21) K. Lewin, R. Lippitt and R. K. White, 1939, 'Patterns of aggressive behaviour in experimentally created social climates', *J. soc. Psych.*, **10**, 271–99.

(22) 'The Antithetical Meaning of Primal Words' (1910), *Standard Edition*, Vol. 11, pp. 153–62.

(23) Words also change their meaning within the time-span of the known history of language. 'Self-conscious' implied originally only self-awareness; now it means unsure of oneself; the German 'selbstbewusst' implies, in contrast, proud of oneself.

(24) *The Interpretation of Dreams* (1900), *Standard Edition*, Vol. 5, p. 353.

(25) H. Hartmann, 'On Parapraxes in the Korsakoff Psychosis' (1924) in H. Hartmann, *Essays on Ego Psychology* (London, The Hogarth Press; New York, International Universities Press, 1964).

(26) H. Ellenberger, *op. cit.*, pp. 506–7; Freud mentions several predecessors too.

(27) *The Interpretation of Dreams* (1900), *Standard Edition*, Vol. 5, pp. 536–7.

(28) *Op. cit.*, pp. 598–9. Joan Wynn Reeves in her excellent book *Thinking About Thinking* (London, Secker & Warburg, 1965), traces five different connotations of the term 'wish' in *The Interpretation of Dreams*.

(29) *Op. cit.*, p. 537.

(30) *Op. cit.*, pp. 539–40.

(31) *Standard Edition*, Vol. 19.

(32) Quoted in J. W. Reeves, *op. cit.*, p. 85 and p. 92.

(33) See, e.g., Martin Mayman (ed), *Psychoanalytic Research, Three Approaches to the Experimental Study of the Subliminal Process* (1973), *Psychological Issues*, Monograph 30.

(34) Ernest R. Hilgard, 'A Neodissociation Interpretation of Pain Reduction in Hypnosis' (1973), *Psych. Review*, Vol. 80, No. 5, 396–411.

(35) *Thinking About Thinking*, *op. cit.*

(36) Heinz Hartmann, *Essays on Ego Psychology*, *op. cit.*, p. 59.

(37) Some psychologists agree. Not only Joan W. Reeves, but also U. Neisser in his *Cognitive Psychology* (New York, Appleton-Century-Crofts, 1967).

(38) H. Ellenberger, *op. cit.*, p. 493.

(39) *Standard Edition*, Vol. 6.

(40) *Standard Edition*, Vol. 8.

(41) In this context it is of some interest that when the love–hate relationship between Freud and Jung approached its dramatic climax Freud drew Jung's attention to an ominous slip in disclaiming that he, Jung, was the defectors' friend. Jung meant to write he was not 'their' (ihr) friend; he wrote 'your' (Ihr) friend. Jung's response was explosive. See William McGuire, ed, *The Freud/Jung Letters* (New Jersey, Princeton University Press, 1974; London, Routledge & Kegan Paul and The Hogarth Press).

(42) *The Psychopathology of Everyday Life* (1901), *Standard Edition*, Vol. 6, pp. 242–3.

(43) F. Bartlett, *Remembering* (Cambridge University Press, 1932).

(44) *Standard Edition*, Vol. 2, p. 300.

(45) *Standard Edition*, Vol. 14, p. 186. The culprit quoting out of context here is F. Cioffi, in Borger and Cioffi, *op. cit.*, p. 493.

(46) Jaques Hadamard, *The Psychology of Invention in the Mathematical Field* (Oxford University Press, 1945). W. I. B. Beveridge, *The Art of Scientific Investigation* (New York, Norton, 1951), contains several additional examples.

(47) *Standard Edition*, Vol. 18.

CHAPTER 4

(1) H. Hartmann, *Essays on Ego Psychology*, *op. cit.*, p. 324.

(2) J. Lacan, *The Language of the Self*, translated by A. Wilden (Johns Hopkins Press, 1969).

(3) L. von Bertalanffy, *Problems of Life* (New York, Wiley, 1952), p. 134.

(4) Freud developed his second view of personality in his last major theoretical work, *The Ego and the Id*, in 1923 (*Standard Edition*, Vol. 19). A shorter version of this theory is contained in Lecture 31 of the *New Introductory Lectures*, 'The Dissection of the Psychical Personality' (1932), *Standard Edition*, Vol. 22.

(5) See Note 39 in Chapter 2.

(6) Joan W. Reeves, *op. cit.*, p. 163.

(7) Gordon W. Allport, *Pattern and Growth in Personality* (New York, Holt, Rinehart & Winston, 1961).

(8) George Kelly, *The Psychology of Personal Constructs* (New York, Norton, 1955).

(9) Whitney J. Oates (ed), *Basic Writings of Saint Augustine* (New York, Random House, 1948). See also I. Chein, *The Science of Behaviour and the Image of Man* (London, Tavistock, 1972), pp. 59–63, which deals

with cause and purpose, implicitly based on the same conception of time in psychology which Augustine expressed by the idea of a three-fold present.

(10) 'The Dissection of the Psychical Personality' (1932), *Standard Edition*, Vol. 22.

(11) 'Character and Anal Erotism' (1908), *Standard Edition*, Vol. 9.

(12) See in this context R. S. Peters, *The Concept of Motivation*, 1958, whose lucid analysis of confusion in various psychological theories about the concept of motivation is important far beyond this point.

(13) Quoted in D. P. Kimble, *Physiological Psychology* (Addison-Wesley, 1963).

(14) 'The Dissection of the Psychical Personality', *op. cit.*

(15) Gilbert Ryle, *The Concept of Mind* (London, Hutchinson, 1949).

(16) 'The Dissection of the Psychical Personality', *op. cit.*

(17) Leon Festinger, *A Theory of Cognitive Dissonance* (New York, Harper Row, 1957).

(18) F. C. Bartlett, *Remembering* (Cambridge University Press, 1932).

(19) 'The Dissection of the Psychical Personality', *op. cit.*

(20) *Ibid.*

(21) K. Pawlick and R. B. Cattell, 'Third-order Factors in Objective Personality Tests', *Br. J. Psychol.* (1964), **55**, 1–18.

(22) In Chicago Institute for Psychoanalysis (ed), *The Annual of Psychoanalysis*, Vol. 1, 1973 (New York, Quadrangle), Michael F. Basch, 'Psychoanalysis and Theory Formation', pp. 39–52.

(23) 'The Dissection of the Psychical Personality', *op. cit.*

(24) *Ibid.*

CHAPTER 5

(1) See, for example, the first and last paragraph of Lecture XX, entitled 'The Sexual Life of Human Beings' (1917), *Standard Edition*, Vol. 16. Apparently Freud wrote these lectures verbatim, before delivering them from memory.

(2) See Christopher Lasch's review essay, 'Freud and Women', *The New York Review*, 3 October, 1974, for a discussion of the general issue; and Juliet Mitchell, *Psychoanalysis and Feminism* (London, Allen Lane, 1974) for the most thoughtful example of a pro-Freudian feminist position.

(3) *New Introductory Lectures*, Lecture 33, 'Femininity' (1932), *Standard Edition*, Vol. 22.

(4) Freud has been accused of having appropriated, without acknowledgement, the idea of bi-sexuality indirectly from Otto Weininger (through W. Fliess), a mad and brilliant young man who committed

suicide soon after the publication of his book *Geschlecht und Charakter.* See also Ellenberger, *op. cit.,* p. 545.

(5) See Chapter 2 for the controversy about Freud's ideas on infantile sexuality.

(6) George S. Klein, 'Freud's Two Theories of Sexuality', Chapter 5 in Louis Breger, ed, *Clinical-Cognitive Psychology: Models and Integrations* (New York, Prentice-Hall, 1970). I am deeply indebted to this essay for my understanding of Freud.

(7) *Three essays on the theory of sexuality* (1905), *Standard Edition,* Vol. 7.

(8) Philip Rieff, *op. cit.*

(9) Schorske, *op. cit.,* p. 344.

(10) Paul Ricoeur, *Freud and Philosophy,* an essay on interpretation, translated by Denis Savage (Yale University Press, 1970), p. 516.

(11) *Standard Edition,* Vol. 9, 1908.

(12) 'Analysis of a Phobia in a Five-Year-Old Boy' (1909), *Standard Edition,* Vol. 10.

(13) 'Femininity', *op. cit.*

(14) Freud observed in himself significant changes during adulthood. For evidence, see *Origins of Psychoanalysis, op. cit.,* and *An Autobiographical Study, op. cit.*

(15) Paul Kline, *op. cit.*

(16) *Standard Edition,* Vol. 22, p. 135.

(17) *Femininity and Psychoanalysis, op. cit.*

(18) Freud was exceedingly reticent about his own sex life. There is, however, in the Freud/Jung letters, *op. cit.,* an indication that his active sex life did not outlast middle age.

(19) Outstanding among them his sister-in-law, Lou Andreas-Salomé, and the Princess Marie Bonaparte.

(20) *Standard Edition,* Vol. 23.

(21) It should be clear, however, that the slow development of the human child is an advantage of inestimable value because it provides a period for learning; an evolutionary reversal toward a shortening of the child's biological, social and cultural dependency would hardly be adaptive since it would leave less time for learning the culture. Yet it should be noted that there are some signs which indicate a shortening of the dependency period, e.g. the earlier onset of puberty in the Western World, a widespread and systematic trend over the decades of this century.

(22) Martin Freud, in *Reflected Glory, op. cit.,* e.g. mentions Freud's support for the reactionary Schuschnigg regime in Austria which preceded Hitler's invasion.

(23) *Standard Edition*, Vol. 9.

(24) *Standard Edition*, Vol. 9, p. 199.

(25) This was certainly the situation for the Viennese middle class. Freud had no contact with the dilemmas of working-class young men and women.

(26) *Civilization and its Discontents* (1929), *Standard Edition*, Vol. 21.

(27) 'Sexuality in the Aetiology of the Neuroses' (1898), *Standard Edition*, Vol. 3.

(28) 'A Study in Social Myth', *American Psychologist*, July 1975. Here is an uncompromising anti-Freudian view.

(29) I am fully aware of the possibility that this critique of Freud may well stem from my own bias in being a woman. Indeed, it is doubtful whether any systematic thought is ever produced without the stimulant of such personal involvement. It is the examination of the logic of the argument and counter-argument which in the end decides where a personal bias is constructive or where destructive.

(30) See the excellent discussion of the limits of reductionism from psychology to physiology in Margaret Boden, *The Concept of Purpose in Psychology* (Harvard University Press, 1972).

CHAPTER 6

(1) *The Origins of Psycho-Analysis*, *op. cit.*, p. 246.

(2) Jones, *op. cit.*, Vol. 2, reports that Freud had actually written twelve papers in that series in a very short period, but had apparently seen fit to publish only five, 'Instincts and Their Vicissitudes', 'Repression', 'The Unconscious', 'Metapsychological Supplement to the Theory of Dreams', and 'Mourning and Melancholia', all in *Standard Edition*, Vol. 14, while apparently destroying the others, of which only five titles remain: 'Consciousness', 'Anxiety', 'Conversion Hysteria', 'Obsessional Neuroses', and 'General Synthesis of Transference Neuroses'.

(3) Jones, *op. cit.*, Vol. 2, p. 185.

(4) Merton M. Gill, ed, *The Collected Papers of David Rapaport* (New York, Basic Books, 1967), pp. 795–6.

(5) David Rapaport, 'The Structure of Psychoanalytic Theory: a Systematising Attempt', in S. Koch, ed, *Psychology: A Study of a Science*, Vol. III (New York, McGraw-Hill, 1959).

(6) Heinz Hartmann, *Essays on Ego Psychology*, *op. cit.*, p. 328.

(7) J. Strachey, *Standard Edition*, Vol. 14, p. 105.

(8) Ernest R. Hilgard, 'The Scientific Status of Psychoanalysis', in E. Nagel et al., eds, *Logic, Methodology and Philosophy of Science* (Stanford University Press 1962).

(9) J. Laplanche and J. B. Pontalis, *The Language of Psycho-Analysis* (London, Hogarth, 1973; New York, Norton), p. 249.

(10) Heinz Hartmann, *op. cit.*, p. 322.

(11) *The Origins of Psycho-Analysis, op. cit.*, p. 22.

(12) See M. Masud R. Khan's brief but poignant editorial preface to Laplanche and Pontalis, *op. cit.*

(13) Quoted in Merton M. Gill, *op. cit.*, p. 799.

(14) In Merton M. Gill, *op. cit.*, pp. 853–915.

(15) Heinz Hartmann, *op. cit.*, p. 43.

(16) *Standard Edition*, Vol. 18.

(17) 'Instincts and Their Vicissitudes' (1915), *Standard Edition*, Vol. 14.

(18) In Merton M. Gill, *op. cit.*, p. 857.

(19) Dalbir Bindra and Jane Stewart, eds, *Motivation*, 2nd ed (Penguin, 1971), p. 9.

(20) Laplanche and Pontalis, *op. cit.*, p. 127.

(21) *Standard Edition*, Vol. 18, pp. 30–31.

(22) *Standard Edition*, Vol. 17, p. 118.

(23) Laplanche and Pontalis, *op. cit.*, have dealt informatively and critically with the inconsistencies and difficulties of Freud's energy concepts. See particularly their article on the Principle of Constancy.

(24) In Louis Breger, ed, *Clinical-Cognitive Psychology: Models and Integrations* (New York, Prentice-Hall, 1969), Chapter 5.

(25) Paul Ricoeur, *op. cit.*, p. 424.

(26) *Ibid.*, p. 457.

(27) Leon Festinger, *A Theory of Cognitive Dissonance* (Row Peterson, 1957).

(28) See Freud, 'Psycho-analytic Notes on an Autobiographical Account of a Case of Paranoia (dementia paranoides)', *Standard Edition*, Vol. 12, but also Morton Schatzman, *Soul Murder, Persecution in the Family* (Allen Lane, 1973). Schatzman presents fascinating material showing how Schreber's father advocated in general, and practised in particular against his two sons, the most brutal repressive child rearing methods. Paternal threat and persecution were here not phantasy but real events which Freud did not know about. However, Schatzman's critique of Freud's interpretation of the case seems misplaced. Whether real or imagined persecution in childhood, Schreber's adult symptoms are still adequately described as a withdrawal of libido from the external world; his convictions, while insane, about his intercourse with God were not based on conscious memory of his tortured childhood.

(29) R. Joynson, 'The Return of Mind', *Bull. Br. Psycho. Soc.* (1971)

NOTES

(30) *Standard Edition*, Vol. 23, p. 197.

(31) Jean-Paul Sartre, *'Mauvaise Foi* and the Unconscious', p. 78 in Richard Wollheim, ed, *Freud, A Collection of Critical Essays* (New York, Anchor Books, 1974).

(32) Ernest Hilgard, 'A Neodissociation Interpretation of Pain Reduction in Hypnosis', *Psych. Review* (1973), **80** (5), 396–411.

(33) *Standard Edition*, Vol. 19.

(34) Heinz Hartmann, *op. cit.*, pp. 43–4.

(35) Thomas S. Kuhn, *The Structure of Scientific Revolutions*, 2nd ed (University of Chicago Press, 1962).

(36) M. Foucault, *The Order of Things: An Archeology of the Human Sciences* (London, Tavistock, 1970).

(37) *Standard Edition*, Vol. 7, p. 201. Note also that Freud repeatedly used the opportunity offered by his children and grandchildren for psychological observation, vide examples of children's dreams in *The Interpretation of Dreams*, and the 'Fort-Da' example in *Beyond the Pleasure Principle*.

(38) *Standard Edition*, Vol. 7, p. 239.

(39) See, e.g., G. Allport, *Personality* (Henry Holt, 1937).

(40) H. Hartmann, *op. cit.*, pp. 221–2.

(41) In Merton M. Gill, *op. cit.*, p. 806.

(42) D. Rapaport, 'The Structure of Psychoanalytic Theory', *Psych. Issues*, **6** (1960).

(43) *Standard Edition*, Vol. 21, pp. 59–145.

(44) *Standard Edition*, Vol. 21.

(45) *Standard Edition*, Vol. 21.

CHAPTER 7

(1) See, e.g. his statements about colleagues in his correspondence with Jung, McGuire (ed), *op. cit.*, or his statement in his 'A Short Account of Psychoanalysis' (1923), *Standard Edition*, Vol. 19, in talking about Jung's and Adler's defections, that the majority of his co-workers 'remained firm and continued their work along the lines indicated to them'. See also Lou Andreas-Salomé, *In der Schule bei Freud* (Max Niehans, 1958).

(2) *Standard Edition*, Vol. 19, pp. 108–40.

(3) O. Pötzl (1917) translated into English 1960, 'The Relationship between Experimentally Induced Dream Images and Indirect Vision', *Psych. Issues*, Monograph 7, 41–120 (New York, International Universities Press). For further work in this area see *Psychol. Issues*, Monograph 30, 1973.

(4) 'Constructions in Analysis' (1937), *Standard Edition*, Vol. 23.

(5) 'From the History of an Infantile Neurosis' (1914), *Standard Edition*, Vol. 17.

(6) See, e.g. Stuart W. Cook and Claire Selltiz, 'A multiple indicator approach to attitude measurement', *Psych. Bull*, A.P.A., 1964, Vol. 62.

(7) *Standard Edition*, Vol. 2, p. 9.

(8) *Standard Edition*, Vol. 10.

(9) *Standard Edition*, Vol. 10, pp. 344ff.

(10) *Standard Edition*, Vol. 7.

(11) *Standard Edition*, Vol. 22, Lecture 34.

(12) A. Flew (1956) 'Motives and the Unconscious'. In H. Feigl and M. Scriven, eds, *The Foundations of Science and the Concepts of Psychology and Psychoanalysis* (University of Minnesota Press).

(13) Jürgen Habermas (1968), *Knowledge and Human Interests* (New York, Beacon Press, 1971), pp. 162ff.

(14) Lee J. Cronbach, 'Beyond the Two Disciplines of Scientific Psychology', *American Psychologist* (Feb, 1975), **30** (2), 125.

(15) E.g. *Standard Edition*, Vol. 14, p. 39. Freud dealt there with the criticism that psychoanalysis was nothing but the outgrowth of the sensuality and immorality of the Vienna milieu by saying that Vienna was in that respect not different from other cities, and by pointing to a logical flaw in the argument: unbridled sexuality should counteract the formation of a theory to which repression was central.

(16) The essay, 'A Child is Being Beaten: A Contribution to the Study of The Origin of Sexual Perversion' (1919), *Standard Edition*, Vol. 17, for example, makes the point indirectly that a search for a common origin of perversions is justified if not one but six patients independently of each other confess to a phantasy of watching a child being beaten.

(17) See, e.g. the literature chapter in *The Interpretation of Dreams* (1900), *Standard Edition*, Vol. 4.

(18) Lecture 31, *Standard Edition*, Vol. 22.

(19) *Standard Edition*, Vol. 20.

(20) Charles Rycroft, *A Critical Dictionary of Psycho-Analysis* (London, Nelson, 1968), pp. xii–xiii.

(21) *Standard Edition*, Vol. 17, pp. 125–34.

(22) *Standard Edition*, Vol. 23.

(23) *Standard Edition*, Vol. 17.

(24) *Standard Edition*, Vol. 13.

(25) Isaiah Berlin, *The Hedgehog and the Fox* (London, Weidenfeld and Nicolson, 1953). The essay is careful to demonstrate that hedgehogs,

e.g. Dante, are neither better nor worse than foxes, e.g. Shakespeare, and proceeds to describe Tolstoi as a fox by nature who thought, however, that being a hedgehog was superior.

(26) *Standard Edition*, Vol. 17, pp. 257–66.

(27) *Standard Edition*, Vol. 13, pp. 1–233.

(28) *Ibid.*, p. 35.

(29) *Standard Edition*, Vol. 23, pp. 3–140.

CHAPTER 8

(1) Lancelot L. Whyte, *The Unconscious Before Freud* (London, Tavistock Publications, 1962), p. viii.

(2) *Standard Edition*, Vol. 18.

(3) C. Hovland, I. Janis and H. H. Kelley, *Communication and Persuasion* (Yale University Press, 1953).

(4) See Chapter 4.

(5) Whyte, *op. cit.*, p. x.

(6) An excellent collection of articles, many of which trace direct intellectual influences on Freud, is contained in: John E. Gedo and George H. Pollock, eds, *Freud: The Fusion of Science and Humanism* (New York, International Universities Press, 1976), *Psych. Issues*, Monograph 34/35.

(7) M. Dorer, *Historische Grundlagen der Psychoanalyse* (Leipzig, 1932).

(8) Whyte, *op. cit.*, p. 63.

(9) *Ibid.*, pp. 94–5.

(10) *Ibid.*, p. 96.

(11) *Ibid.*, p. 102.

(12) *Ibid.*, pp. 149–50; see also Ellenberger, *op. cit.*, pp. 207–8.

(13) *Ibid.*, p. 170.

(14) Ellenberger, *op. cit.*, particularly pp. 3–47. Much of the following section is based on this outstanding book.

(15) Hendrik K. M. Ruitenbeek, *Freud and America* (New York, 1966).

(16) S. Ferenczi, *Further Contributions to the Theory and Technique of Psycho-analysis* (London, Hogarth, 1952). Quoted from Norman O. Brown, *Life Against Death* (London, Routledge & Kegan Paul, 1959).

(17) Whyte, *op. cit.*, p. 177.

(18) *Ibid.*, p. 180.

(19) Norman O. Brown, *op. cit.*

(20) Herbert Marcuse, *Eros and Civilisation* (London, Abacus, 1972).

(21) Ellenberger, *op. cit.*, p. 549.

(22) *Ibid.*, p. 550.

CHAPTER 9

(1) See Neil Warren's thoughtful critique of such assertions in his article 'Is a Scientific Revolution Taking Place in Psychology?—Doubts and Reservations', *Science Studies*, **1**, 407–13.

(2) See M. Jahoda, 'The Migration of Psychoanalysis: Its Impact on American Psychology', in D. Flemming and B. Bailyn (eds), *Perspectives in American History*, Vol. II, 1968, for some similarities and differences between behaviourism and psychoanalysis and for Watson's ambivalence towards Freud.

(3) Ellenberger, *op. cit.*, p. 809.

(4) Margaret Boden, *Purposive Explanation in Psychology* (Harvard University Press, 1972).

(5) Karl R. Popper, *The Logic of Scientific Discovery* (London, Methuen, 1959), p. 280.

(6) Donald T. Campbell, 'On the Conflicts Between Biological and Social Evolution and Between Psychology and Moral Tradition', *American Psychologist* (December 1975), **30**, 1120–21. Note that Campbell's emerging new conception of psychology permits him to quote Freud without attack or defence. This important articles goes beyond the passage quoted and in very different directions, some of which seem to me to have sinister implications.

(7) Merton M. Gill and Philip S. Holzman, eds, *Psychology Versus Metapsychology: Psychoanalytic Essays in Memory of George S. Klein* (New York, International Universities Press, 1976, Monograph 36). This excellent volume contains contributions from psychoanalysts and psychoanalytically trained psychologists both for and against Freud's metapsychology; however, the editors leave the issue unresolved.

(8) Hans Herma, Ernst Kris and Joel Shor, 'Freud's Theory of the Dream in American Textbooks', *J. of Abnorm. and Social Psych* (1943), **38** (3).

(9) Jerome S. Bruner, 'The Freudian Conception of Man and the Continuity of Nature', in Gerald Holton, ed, *Science and the Modern Mind* (New York, Beacon Press, 1958).

(10) Morris R. Cohen and Ernest Nagel, *An Introduction to Logic and Scientific Method* (New York, Harcourt Brace, 1934), p. 192.

(11) Paul Horst, Social Science Research Council Bulletin No. 48, U.S.A. An even more shocking attitude to the first descriptive step in the application of the scientific method to psychological research was revealed in a fairly recent report in a reputable journal of an experiment which manipulated attitudes to the police. The authors reported in a footnote that two subjects in their sample had to be excluded because it was discovered that they actually had developed attitudes to the police.

NOTES

(12) *Standard Edition*, Vol. 17.

(13) Egon Brunswick, *Perception and the Representative Design of Psychological Experiments* (University of California Press, 1956).

(14) S. Koch, ed, *Psychology as a Science*, Vol. 3, Epilogue, pp. 783–6 (New York, McGraw-Hill, 1959).

(15) J. Lacan, *The Language of the Self*, translated by A. Wilden (Johns Hopkins Press, 1968).

(16) See, e.g. M. Brewster Smith, 'Attitude Change', in David L. Sills (ed), *International Encyclopedia of the Social Sciences* (New York, Crowell, Collier, Macmillan, 1968), Vol. 1.

(17) See Paul F. Lazarsfeld's preface to M. Jahoda, P. F. Lazarsfeld and H. Zeisel (1933), *Marienthal* (Aldine, 1971).

(18) A. R. Luria, *The Mind of a Mnemonist* (Jonathan Cape, 1970); and *The Man with a Shattered World* (Jonathan Cape, 1973).

(19) John Bowlby, *Attachment and Loss* (London, The Hogarth Press, 1969; New York, Basic Books).

(20) It is worth noting that Heinz Hartmann, *op. cit.*, one of the few psychoanalysts who shared Freud's aim of developing psychoanalysis into a general psychology, disagreed with him on this point. Not only did he himself conduct experimental research using psychoanalytic concepts, but he remained throughout his life in close intellectual contact with the developments of psychology.

(21) Ernest Becker, *The Denial of Death* (New York, The Free Press, 1973).

Index of Names

Index of Subjects

INDEX OF SUBJECTS